Conversational Joking

Conversational Joking

Joking

HUMOR IN EVERYDAY TALK

Neal R. Norrick

INDIANA UNIVERSITY PRESS
Bloomington • Indianapolis

The paper used in this publication meets the minimum requirements
of American National Standard for Information Sciences—Permanence
of Paper for Printed Library Materials, ANSI Z39.48-1984.

Manufactured in the United States of America

Library of Congress Cataloging-in-Publication Data

Norrick, Neal R.
    Conversational joking: humor in everyday
talk / Neal R. Norrick.
        p.   cm.
    Includes bibliographical references and index.
    ISBN 0-253-34111-6 (alk. paper)
    1. Wit and humor—History and criticism. 2. Conversation
—Psychological aspects. 3. Wit and humor—Psychological aspects.
I. Title.
PN6147.N65   1993
401'.41—dc20   92-19471

            1   2   3   4   5   97   96   95   94   93

For Corinna,
because she never had one before

Contents

Preface

Haste thee, Nymph, and bring with thee
Jest, and youthful jollity,
Quips and cranks and wanton wiles,
Nods and becks and wreathèd smiles, . . .
Sport that wrinkled Care derides,
And Laughter holding both his sides.
Come, and trip it as you go,
On the light fantastic toe.

John Milton, *L'Allegro* ■

But all joking aside for the moment: This book has taken a long time to reach final form; and I have enjoyed plentiful help along the way. My serious involvement with verbal humor began during preparation for a seminar on linguistic approaches to jokes which I co-directed with Winfried Nöth at the University of Kassel, Germany, in 1982. In the years that followed, my initial interest in theories of humor and recycled jokes gradually shifted to joking in naturally occurring conversation, to the speaker strategies of alluding, punning, and teasing as well as the responses they elicit from hearers, and the total effect of joking on the organization and point of a conversation. In the fall of 1989 I conducted a Ph.D. seminar at Northern Illinois University on the microanalysis of conversation which provided a forum for the discussion of my developing ideas on humor in everyday talk; student comments, presentations, and papers helped clarify my thinking on interactional aspects of joking and its role in conversational organization. I would like to thank students in this seminar as well as those who took my undergraduate honors course that same semester for sharing their recorded conversational data with me, especially Alison Berry, Channing Blair, Mary Jandek, Patty Laverty, Shelley Synovic, Jason Turner, and Than

Than Win. A talk I presented on joking repair in conversation at the 1989 meeting of the Linguistic Society of America in Washington, D.C., also elicited valuable comments from participants.

In May 1990, I was invited to speak on repetition as a conversational joking strategy at an NEH-sponsored colloquium on repetition organized by Barbara Johnstone at Texas A&M University. I am very grateful to Barbara and other participants in the colloquium, particularly Pete Becker and Joel Sherzer, for helping shape my thinking on verbal humor. Then in June, Northern Illinois University granted me a very welcome summer stipendium to research this book, and again, in the spring of 1991, a much appreciated sabbatical leave to produce the original manuscript. During that spring I was fortunate enough to participate in the session on discourse analysis organized by Deborah Tannen at the American Association for Applied Linguistics annual meeting in New York, where I first presented my ideas on the metalingual function of conversational joking. I am indebted to Deborah, Candy Goodwin, Marilyn Merritt, and other participants for their valuable ideas on joking and the metalingual function in conversation generally.

In the summer of 1991 I received generous invitations to lecture on humorous anecdotes in conversation at the Universities of Kassel and Braunschweig in Germany: I would like to express my gratitude to Winfried Nöth and Wolfram Bublitz for their kind hospitality as well as for the interest they and their students showed in my work.

At one time or another, various people have read and commented on portions of this study; I particularly want to thank Andy Gallagher, John Lawson, Ann Litow, Ana Longhini, John Morreall, JoEllen Simpson, and Than Than Win. I am eternally grateful to Barbara Johnstone and Deborah Tannen for reading the entire manuscript and commenting extensively on it. Special thanks go to John Van Dyk for the artwork on the cover. Petra remains a constant source of encouragement and my best adviser, while providing an environment rich in conversational joking, along with the help of Nick and Coco.

Transcription Conventions

The conventions summarized below are discussed in some detail in the section "Recording and transcribing conversation and laughter" in chapter 1.

She's out.	Period shows falling tone in preceding element.
Oh yeah?	Question mark shows rising tone in preceding element.
nine, ten.	Comma indicates a level, continuing intonation.
damn	Italics show heavy stress.
bu- but	A single dash indicates a cutoff.
so, (2.0)	Numbers in parentheses show length of timed pauses.
o(ho)kay	Parentheses also enclose word-internal laughter.
[at all.] [I just]	Aligned brackets enclose simultaneous speech by two or more participants.
says "Oh"	Double quotes mark speech set off from the regular voice of the speaker.
{sigh}	Curly braces enclose comments on inaudible or untranscribable elements of the context.

Conversational Joking

1

Introduction

And how far a body can hear on the water such nights!
I heard people talking at the ferry-landing. I heard
what they said, too—every word of it. One man said
it was getting towards the long days and the short
nights now. T'other one said this warn't one of the
short ones, he reckoned—and then they laughed, and
he said it over again, and they laughed again; then
they waked up another fellow and told him, and
laughed, but he didn't laugh; he ripped out something
brisk, and said let him alone. The first fellow said he
'lowed to tell it to his old woman—she would think
it was pretty good; but he said that warn't nothing to
some things he had said in his time.

Mark Twain, *The Adventures of Huckleberry Finn* ∎

Everyday conversation thrives on wordplay, sarcasm, anecdotes, and jokes. Certainly these forms of humor enliven
conversation, but they also help us break the ice, fill uncomfortable pauses, negotiate requests for favors, and build group
solidarity. So an account of joking will be a fundamental part of
any complete description of conversation. And conversation is
the natural home of punning, allusion, and joking. We understand
these forms of humor only if we can explain their integration
into everyday talk and their functioning in it. This book investigates the various forms of humor in their natural conversational

contexts so as to shed light on the structure and point of both conversation and humor.

Interdisciplinary perspectives on the study of humor have achieved considerable agreement about the techniques of jokes and the causes of mirthful laughter. Linguistically oriented research provides us with a workable model of the internal organization and meaning structure of jokes. And work on narrative has begun to elucidate the performance aspects of joke and anecdote telling. At the same time, recent developments in discourse analysis and linguistic pragmatics have contributed much to our understanding of how conversationalists fit jokes and puns into their ongoing talk, and how recipients react to them. Therefore the time seems ripe to combine these various strands into a coherent perspective on conversational joking.

A description of the syntax and semantics of jokes remains incomplete without an understanding of their interpersonal and social dimensions, which requires an investigation of their real-life contexts. And a consideration of actual conversational interaction is even more central to an account of punning, sarcasm, and mocking. Close attention to humor in everyday talk will lead us to a dynamic description of joking interaction, which considers the position of joking in the organization of conversation as well as the internal organization of the joking performance. It must view joke telling, punning, and teasing in relation to power, solidarity, and social distance, and in light of the principles of politeness and cooperation in order to understand how joking can express aggression yet still build rapport. And it should allow us to formulate and answer other appropriate questions about the functions joking fulfills in conversation.

Jean Paul (Richter) called joking a "disguised priest who weds any couple" (1804, part 2, 44); it will take the joint force of all the theoretical perspectives we can muster to make sense of these unions. What I am suggesting, then, is a marriage of convenience between discourse analysis and humor studies, in hopes that it will yield healthy offspring for both areas of research. Of course, even this happy union is possible only with the support of close relations. In fact, the Conversation Analysis school of thought, which looms so large in discourse analysis today, began as and to some degree remains a branch of sociology on its ethnography side. And humor studies is itself an interdisciplinary field encompassing anthropology, psychology, philosophy, and linguistics. So my proposal really amounts to a new emphasis or perspective on natural conversation, rather than a new interdisciplinary collusion as such. This emphasis results in a book focused on detailed analysis of humorous passages from natural conversation with no sense of urgency about generalizing for the present, especially since much previous work on humor has put forward general claims about its role in everyday talk without examining any real conversational data.

Joking in Context

I would like now to take a first look at a joking episode to give some sense of the complex interrelation of joking and context. The discussion will also serve to indicate the perspective to be developed and the range of issues which come in for attention in the following pages. On a plane loading for the flight from New York to Chicago, several passengers were politely letting each other pass, helping each other stow luggage, find seats, and so on, when a man with an unmistakable New York accent said, "What's everybody being so nice for? We're still in New York." A second man laughed and replied, "Yeah. We'll be back in Chicago soon. Then it'll be okay again," which elicited more general laughter. Now the first speaker may be poking fun at the stereotypical brusqueness of his fellow New Yorkers. And he may be kidding the Chicagoans for their eagerness to be nice. Or he may readily accept both the New York and Chicago stereotypes and the associated behavior patterns as valid, neither good nor bad in their respective places, yet still be joking about the clash of customs: "When in New York, be unfriendly; when in Chicago, be friendly." What is funny then is the application of the Chicago rule while still on New York turf. At least the second speaker seems to take the joke this last way. In any case, the physical closeness and jostling in the narrow airplane aisle, the incompatible politeness systems, and perhaps even some preflight jitters need relief of some sort, and the two speakers latch onto humor as the vehicle of choice, laughing about the ambiguity of the situation itself where neither set of customs clearly holds sway.

To get clear about the importance of context, we might ask what other settings could support this joke. A bus headed to Chicago probably would not do, since the greater distance makes the clash of customs less relevant, and the element of relieving tension before takeoff is absent. A flight from New York to Boston or from Chicago to Dallas does not work either, since the stereotypes are different. Nor can we change the participants. First of all, as Deborah Tannen observes, joking in public with strangers is a standard part of New York conversational style, which means that conversationalists' assumptions about when to joke and with whom must also enter into a complete description of the context. Further, if spoken by the Midwesterner, the first remark becomes an indictment of New Yorkers rather than a comment on a clash of conventions. And this might lead to bad feelings rather than complementary joking. So the context of this joking exchange includes more than the physical setting, the participants, and their reasons for being together, or even the emotional atmosphere; it extends to the social roles the participants present and their interrelations along with their cultural lore about places, customs, and interactions, in this particular case stereotypes about New Yorkers and Chicagoans, the history of rivalry between the two cities, and so on.

Two strangers can exchange and enjoy jokes about their differences only because they share a wealth of background information about their respective habits as well as assumptions about who jokes with whom, where, when, and about what. All this must count as context in the wide sense of how participants in an interaction perceive their situation, goals, and interrelations. The first speaker must signal both a desire to communicate and a humorous tone through a set of hints and cues on a whole range of levels from prosody and phonology through syntax, lexis, and rhythmic organization on up to partially formulaic discourse strategies, as discussed by Gumperz (1982a and 1982b). While the first speaker signals his status as a New Yorker with characteristic accent features, the second underlines his identification as a Chicagoan with the phrases "*back* in Chicago" and "it'll be okay *again*." This points up the function of joking as a means of presenting a self—in the sense of Goffman (1955)—and eliciting social information about others, all of which, in turn, becomes a part of the dynamic context.

Joking allows participants to recognize their respective affiliations and to align themselves in terms of them or in spite of them. Humor provides a socially acceptable vent for hostility toward other people and their idiosyncracies. Thus, in our example, it seems the New Yorker and the Chicagoan align themselves together to laugh about the clash of conventions and those caught in it. Joking and laughing together helps establish rapport and can lead to further involvement. For these two passengers, the preflight negotiation was a potential joking context, and for a couple other passengers—myself included—it was a laughing context, though not everyone laughed who heard the exchange. Perhaps they would have felt uncomfortable laughing with strangers; or they felt the jokes targeted New Yorkers, or Midwesterners; or they failed to get the joke, perhaps because they rejected the relevant stereotypes for whatever reasons. Such speculations about why some listeners laugh while others do not more properly belong to the realm of psychology. What a discourse analysis perspective has to offer is insight into the organization and functioning of joking in the conversational context. And as we are beginning to see, joking allows us to manipulate talk and participants in various ways, by presenting a self, probing for information about the attitudes and affiliations of our interlocutors, realigning ourselves with respect to them, and, of course, injecting humor into a situation, which helps to relieve tension and foster friendly interaction. These functions then reflect back on the context of talk.

The example cited above simplifies the discussion of context and joking in several important ways. First, it includes no *conversational* context, no talk previous to the first joking remark. By contrast, most conversational joking grows out of foregoing talk and much plays on it directly, with punning and repartee as the most obvious examples. Second, because the participants are strangers, they bring with them no past history of joking or any common interaction at all. If the context of joking—and really of any talk exchange—consists in whatever perceptions participants have of their interaction and their relations to each other, then this includes their recollection and evaluation of past encounters and the sorts of joking they have engaged in together. Some individuals joke with almost everyone; some people kid each other whenever they meet; some pairs or larger groups develop "customary joking relationships" in which teasing and joking are habitual and competitive; and these histories of joking have much relevance for any interactions of the people involved. Finally, crucial elements are missing from the context described above, since I wrote down the example from memory after a single, live hearing, rather than from a taped recording, which allows multiple playbacks, detailed transcription, and editing. Timing is crucial in both joking and laughter, so careful attention to the transcript is important. Meticulous transcription and analysis of joking interactions reveal characteristics not noticed otherwise; so nearly all the examples treated below were transcribed from audio recordings, a matter I return to shortly. The ways joking builds on foregoing talk, the nature of what I am calling customary joking relationships, and the details of joking and laughing all play a significant role in the chapters to come, along with the other features of context already mentioned.

What's So Funny?

In the example above, a consideration of the context helped clarify the joking exchange; but we are not always privy to all the contextual background we need to understand a joke. There is often plenty of joking and laughter in any spontaneous conversation. When we are involved in this talk ourselves, we laugh and joke along with the others. But when we observe strangers engaged in mirthful conversation, we may wonder what they are laughing about: What's so funny? Although we understand their words, we feel their amusement must be due to "inside jokes"— jokes only group members have the shared background knowledge to understand. Even when we listen to a recorded conversation of our own played back to us, we are likely to be surprised again why everyone seems so amused. This time the answer must go beyond the recognition of common ground to include various aspects of the particular momentary context.

Freud (1905) maintained that laughing together at the same jokes was evidence of a "far-reaching psychical conformity"; and we may imagine that such conformity arises only within a specific interaction and lasts only so long as those particular participants continue their interaction. Folk wisdom admirably encapsulates this recognition in the formula "I guess you had to be there." This saying glosses a number of factors, including the relationships between the participants, their past histories of interaction, the kinds of humor they routinely engage in, the way they frame the immediate context, and the interaction as a whole. All these factors contribute to an understanding of a particular joking exchange in conversation. I will touch on them all at various points in the analyses to come, though I have taken pains to choose accessible examples which we can follow without overly much setup.

It has been common practice in studies of humor to cite examples from anthologies of jokes or literary works *assuming* they were funny and then to explain how they work, why they *are* funny. Yet psychological studies of humor from Freud (1905) onward have stressed the importance of context in determining what we find funny; and experiments have borne them out, as reported in Goldstein and McGhee (1972); Chapman and Foot (1976); McGhee and Goldstein (1983) and references there. La Fave, Haddad, and Maesen (1976) state programmatically that "there are no jokes"—just texts someone has used or may use to get a laugh under the right circumstances. Recall in this regard the popular belief that "some folks can tell 'em, and some can't." Sacks (1973) and Sherzer (1978) show that many puns in conversation go unnoticed.

So even if we identify something said as a pun or joke, how can we tell if it is funny or not? The study of humor in its concrete conversational context helps solve this problem, since, as Feste says in Shakespeare's *Twelfth Night* II iii 49, "present mirth hath present laughter." Jokes and puns call for laughter upon completion; they build a slot for laughter into the structure of the ongoing conversation, which makes us expect laughter and notice its absence. In the passage cited from *Huckleberry Finn* at the outset of this chapter, the original pair of talkers laughed at the clever remark on the length of the night twice, but the third man they awoke did not laugh and "ripped out something brisk" instead. The absence of laughter invites special kinds of inferences, in particular that the recipient failed to get the joke or that the joke failed to amuse the recipient. In order to avoid the former inference, the recipient may respond with the conventional *aw* or a mirthless *ha-ha* to exhibit understanding without amusement. Or the listener may produce an explicit negative evaluation, as the rudely awakened man presumably does with the phrase Huck characterizes as "something brisk." In choosing the conversational excerpts to be cited below, I insisted on these explicit signs that the irony, puns, anecdotes, and jokes were in fact received as funny—or at least as endeavors to be funny. In almost all cases, this means they contained clearly audible laughter, though, inevitably, a few examples elicit only *aw* or a snide comment on the attempted joke. When laughter or one of these other characteristic responses ensues at the appropriate point after a turn containing a recognizable joking structure, it seems reasonable to say the speaker was joking, teasing, playing with words, being sarcastic, or something similar.

Of course, we laugh at all sorts of things besides wordplay and funny stories. Tickling can make us laugh, just as nervousness or embarrassment can (a subject I return to in the next chapter). Some of us may laugh in relief when our misery or fear subsides. Even the laughter of mirth due to humor has been assigned to separate mechanisms by psychologists and philosophers, and their theories fall into three general groups. According to the superiority theory of laughter, most closely associated with Hobbes (1650), we laugh from "sudden glory" at the pratfalls and errors of others because they enhance our feelings of superiority. The so-called relief theory of laughter, which we can let Freud (1905) represent, claims that we laugh due to a saving of psychic energy via the release of repressed emotion. This release is triggered by various techniques, for instance the compression of two words into one "portmanteau word" like *anecdotage*. Koestler (1964) sought to coalesce superiority theories and relief theories in his notion of "bisociation" or simultaneous perception of a single stimulus in two separate frames of reference: See Norrick (1986) for an analysis of these reference frames as cognitive schemas. The identification of bipolar perception as the cause of laughter places Koestler among adherents of the third position, namely incongruity theory, with echoes reaching back at least as far as Kant's *Critique of Judgment* (1790).

Seeking even greater generality, Morreall (1983) proposes that laughter results from a sudden psychological shift, which would account for Hobbesian sudden glory, Freud's release of repressed energy, and Koestler's simultaneous perception within clashing frames, as well as the laughter due to tickling, nervous tension, and relief from strong emotion. It would also encompass Bateson's (1953) analysis of laughter in recognition of a "play frame," since, for Bateson, play involves the paradoxical perception of both a serious message and a metamessage, "this is play," in the same event. So we cannot infallibly reason from laughter to amusement or play just because we identify some laughter as a sign of them. Especially Jefferson (1979; 1984a; 1985) has concerned herself with the placement of all kinds of laughter in conversation and their organizational implications, but see Schenkein (1972) for related discussion. Nevertheless, a close analysis of context, including the precise placement of laughter, should always make it clear when participants are laughing in response to a word, phrase, turn, or narrative which strikes them as funny. Careful attention to the transcription conventions outlined in the next section will help us in this endeavor.

Recording and Transcribing Conversation and Laughter

Most of the discussion below focuses on excerpts from real conversations among family members and friends, fellow students and colleagues. The conversations were recorded and transcribed by my students and me, usually for projects unrelated to the present goal of analyzing verbal humor. We always secured permission to tape the interactions beforehand, and placed our recorders in view of everyone present. More often than not, we were ourselves participants in the conversations we recorded; but I have subsequently assigned fictional names to all participants to preserve anonymity for everyone involved, as promised. These names differ in some cases from pseudonyms I used for these same speakers in excerpts from this data base analyzed in earlier talks and publications. Almost all my own recordings were completed some time before I began to think about investigating conversational joking as such, and I have chosen examples where my own joking contributions were marginal.

All the participants are native-born white Anglo-Americans, but for one culturally and linguistically assimilated resident from northern Europe, now all living just west of Chicago. I will give pertinent background information about the participants in particular exchanges as they appear, especially in cases of longer excerpts and connected passages. Despite the obvious cultural bias inherent in this—or any—corpus of conversational humor, I hope to have selected examples of jokes and anecdotes resembling those my readers are used to hearing and telling, and I trust that the illustrations of banter and wordplay will recall humorous strategies most readers recognize and use themselves.

Of course, the transcribed jokes are not as polished as the thoroughly practiced materials of professional comedians, and the banter will certainly be less clever than the wordplay we find in literary works or anthologies of witticisms. But these real-life passages have a genuine personal validity lacking in carefully authored and edited texts. Close attention to the sequencing and effects of real, organic conversational humor should yield an *ah-hah* effect as the reader recognizes strategies and habits familiar from personal experience. Consequently, I will not be overly eager to generalize from the particular examples to abstract rules or hypotheses. The data speaks eloquently for itself in many cases. It provides ample evidence that joking grows from and thrives in the concrete conversational context; it brings out the interactive nature of joking and the central role of the audience; and it serves as a natural antidote to the over-rich diet of carefully selected, written, literary humor we have consumed in the past.

On the down side, for readers unaccustomed to it, transcribed conversation initially appears rather jumbled and chaotic on the page. We are of course perfectly at home conversing, and usually even when listening to recorded conversation, but everyday talk takes on a foreign aspect when transcribed. Self-correction, interruption, listener feedback, and simultaneous talk all make a conversational transcript less linear and fluent than the carefully marshaled paragraphs of an essay and less orderly than the artificially discrete speeches assigned to successive characters in a play script. I have simplified the transcriptions where the minutiae of timing and overlap were irrelevant to the point being made, but often such details can be quite revealing. For instance, precisely the onset of laughter by various participants tells us much about the presentation and reception of a pun or joke, and the particulars of audience participation correlate in interesting ways with the difference between canned narrative jokes and spontaneous personal anecdotes. Hence, in many instances, I opt for fairly detailed transcriptions with as much setup and explication as seems necessary. The effort we invest in careful transcription and close attention to details of the performance and reaction to conversational humor repays the reader many times over in the insight so gained.

No system of transcription is perfect. Any set of conventions represents a compromise between accuracy and readability, between standard orthography and special symbols. I use regular spelling with appropriate contractions for normal-speed casual talk even when an eye-dialect spelling like *hafta* or *gotcha* comes closer to the actual pronunciation than *have to* or *got you* respectively. This lets me reserve such markers for especially rapid and exaggeratedly careless speech, where they signal a style switch by the speaker as part of dramatization in a narrative or roleplay in sarcasm. The only exception I have made to this rule is the rather frequent single unit *y'know,* which must remain distinct from the two-word phrase *you know* to avoid confusion.

Italic print highlights stressed syllables, whether produced with a higher pitch, greater volume, a longer vowel, or some combination of these devices. Even in emphatic speech, conversationalists usually only stress a single syllable in an utterance, which I represent as "That's *won*derful"; whereas "That's *wonderful*" would indicate all three syllables of *wonderful* received special stress about equally.

A single dash directly after a letter or word signifies an abrupt cutoff, typically when a speaker hears interrupting talk or wants to rephrase a sentence in progress, as in:

FRANK: With a little- with some herbs.

A pause of a second or more appears as an appropriate number of seconds and tenths in parentheses:

TRUDY: Next time, (1.0) a little purple maybe.

Periods, question marks, and commas indicate intonation units, rather than complete declarative and interrogative sentences or pauses. Thus a period shows a final falling contour, not necessarily a complete sentence, as in the passage below on Ned's initial *No* and on *well* in Frank's second turn. A comma indicates a level, continuing intonation, as we see on several words after the *well,* as Frank puts together a halting, but clearly ongoing statement. And a question mark indicates a final rise, an intonation which expects a response, though not necessarily a real question like Ned's *Have you?:* Thus the rising contour on *minute* shown by the question mark conveys a lack of certainty, rather than a request for confirmation, as we see in Frank's continuation with a dependent clause.

FRANK: Have you ever seen this *Simp*sons thing?
NED: No. Have you?
FRANK: I *think* I well. I, I saw it, for, I guess, a minute? When I first heard them yelling about it.

The representation of laughter presents special problems. Simply writing *Al: Laughs* loses sight of conversational dynamics and prosodic features such as the duration and intonation of the laughter, its overlap with speech or laughter of others. And it fails to capture the quality of the laughter, which can range from a nasal exhalation at the end of a word, rendered as *Okaybb,* to a booming *ba ba ba.* In the spirit of Jefferson (1979; 1984a; 1985), I will try to approximate these distinct varieties as closely as possible within the normal orthographic conventions of English. Finally, laughter often initiates a word or occurs word-internally; such laughter I place in parentheses to distinguish it from the word itself, as in the utterance represented below.

FRED: (h)Tha(ha)t's (h)all (h)ri(hi)ght he he.

The final *he he* is separated from the word *right* to indicate that it is audible as a separate item rather than as aspiration tacked onto and within the stress pattern of the word itself.

Simultaneous speech is quite common in everyday conversation. For one thing, listeners typically intersperse attention signals like *uh-huh* and *yeah* and evaluative comments like *really?* and *you don't say* in ongoing talk by others. In conversation filled with joking, laughter often takes the place of other signals to show attention and appreciation. And besides laughter overlapping with speech, we regularly find simultaneous stretches of laughter. Also, a second speaker may begin to talk during a pause, only to have the first speaker continue at the same time. And genuine interruptions also occur. Especially in joking interactions, a second speaker is more likely to break into ongoing talk to make a funny comment. I use sets of square brackets aligned at the left end to enclose overlapping sequences of all these kinds. Thus in the first exchange below, Vera begins her comment at a potential utterance completion point, though Jim goes on to another clause before stopping, so they end up speaking simultaneously.

> JIM: and we'd lie on the back lawn
>   [and pretend to be flying and stuff.]
> VERA: [The basis of true love. Yes.]

And the next sequence shows Leona laughing at the first clause Sally produces, then right through to the end of the second, at which point she begins speaking herself.

> SALLY: He'll tell Mary and
>   [Mary will tell Mike.]
> LEONA: [Huhhuhhuh.] Mary will tell Mike hehaha.

Even this extension and enrichment of our standard orthography cannot provide a complete description of the actual audible performance, especially since conversational joking often involves regional dialect features and parodies of foreign accents; voices, squeals, and shouts to suggest another person, a different group, the other gender; imitated sounds of animals, car brakes, doorbells and the like; to say nothing of facial expressions, gazes, gestures, and other actions in the visual domain which do not show up at all on audio tape. I will use double quotes to mark speech produced in a manner which sets it off from the regular voice of the speaker, whether it turns out to be an actual recognizable quote or, rather, a parody of a person, text, or style identified somehow in the context. Thus in the passage below, Jim dramatizes his own youthful reaction in a whiney voice to recall an earlier stage in his life.

> JIM: Y'know to see what it was like.
> And "I don't see how you *use* this."

Curly braces are used for comments on voice characterizations, sound effects, and contextual information where appropriate, but, unavoidably, much remains for the reader to supply through empathy and imagination. A brief summary of these transcription conventions appears in the preliminary pages.

Classes and Functions

My initial scholarly interest in humor focused on recycled witticisms: proverbial phrases, clichés, one-liners, stock responses, and puns for recurrent situations which we learn and repeat verbatim. When I started to look at creative wordplay and spontaneous narratives, I felt the distinction between recycled and original humor was basic and would prove to be the central element of classification in a study like this. But the distinction becomes blurred in the case of personal anecdotes we tell, retell, and embellish from one conversation to the next; and it creates problems for the classification of allusions. These problems multiply when the allusion fits its context via punning, as when a friend I will call Ray commented on a recipe for tofu potato casserole by saying "That's like the bland leading the bland." Now Ray was certainly conscious of the original formula in which the blind lead the blind, and he may even have previously heard the phrase with the punning substitution of *bland,* though pretty certainly not with reference to potatoes and tofu, so his remark was formulaic, and perhaps doubly so, yet original in its application. The more I examined conversational joking, the more I began to see varying degrees of creativity and wordplay in much allusion and re-citation of formulas and phrases from other spoken and written sources. So though I have not entirely abandoned the distinction between formulaic wit and spontaneous joking or between canned jokes and funny anecdotes which arise in context, I hardly feel it provides the principal criterion for classifying examples or organizing discussions in this book.

I also considered organizing my presentation around the various traditionally recognized genres of humor, starting, say, with the narrative joke and working through the anecdote down to repartee and punning, then on to the single-turn forms like hyperbole and irony. Such an order would tend to suggest that the traditional forms are truly separable and discrete—while my real-life examples consistently show them to occupy points on various continua and to occur phenomenally in mixed and hybrid forms. Of course, it would be quite surprising if spontaneous conversational joking fit neatly into classes initially recognized for literary work, but in fact even real literary examples fit the schematization just as poorly. Occasionally writers like Brown (1956) have proposed taxonomies for puns, while others like Redfern (1984) have wisely eschewed such attempts, and Nash (1985) has stressed the mutability and organic relationship between humorous forms. Furthermore, a form-based classification would emphasize form and lose sight of function, which fails to reflect the reality of the concrete joking context. The form or genre of an example of humor, say its classification as a joke versus an anecdote, manifests itself most saliently in the preface it receives and the sort of audience participation and response it elicits in the conversational context, so that form follows function rather than conversely, as we shall see repeatedly in the chapters to come. Hence it seemed most practical to let function dictate the classification and treatment of examples.

It is fine to invoke the notion of function, except that there is scant agreement on just what kinds of functions are involved and on which levels. For the present purpose of exploring the role of joking in conversation, I first oriented my thinking toward the level of function identified by Jakobson (1960) for speech focused on the six basic components of the communication event. Jakobson recognized an "emotive" function for speech directed at the speaker's mental state, a "conative" function for speech directed at hearer response, a "referential" one for that directed at states of affairs in the external world, a "metalingual" for that directed at the code in use, a "phatic" at the channel of contact, and a "poetic" at the form of the message itself. The schematization of functions proposed by Halliday (1976; 1978) reflects a slightly higher level of abstraction, and also partly meshes with my categories. In addition, Hymes (1962; 1972) has had much to do with my understanding of Jakobson, and my notion of function here as well.

My focus on natural conversation forces me to think in terms of observable features of the concrete context. And this leads me to feel that the "organizational" function should receive attention before we go on to the others. This organizational function corresponds roughly to Jakobson's phatic function of speech focused on contact. For us, this will mean focus on the conversational interaction as such, which comes quite close to Halliday's "textual" function. It includes such general matters as getting talk going, keeping it moving, changing its direction, winding back down, and so on, but also our concern with the micro-level of the individual utterance pair, such as call and response, question and answer. For example, the organizational dimension of greeting new arrivals to a group with a joking expression like "Look what the cat drug in" might involve changing the current topic, realigning the group, and opening the floor to the new participants.

Once we have oriented ourselves to the organization and workings of conversation, we can move on to what I will call the "interpersonal dimension" of joking. I borrow the expression *interpersonal* and much of its content from Halliday, though again my emphasis on conversation seems to broaden the term. Certainly, my discussion goes beyond the hearer-directed conative focus of Jakobson to incorporate most of what his speaker-oriented emotive focus does, since I am concerned precisely with the *inter*personal, that is with the speaker's presentation of a personality through the joke performance and the elicitation of action from and information about the hearer. A lot of what

I want to get at in my discussion of the interpersonal dimension grows out of work on social interaction by Goffman, and research on politeness, solidarity, and rapport by Lakoff, Brown and Levinson, and Tannen. The interpersonal dimension of the jocular greeting "Look what the cat drug in" would include integrating the new arrivals into the group already present as people who belong—the kind of people we can joke around with.

This discussion merges naturally into a consideration of the metalingual focus, where talk revolves around the form of talk itself; and here I follow Jakobson entirely. Participants in conversational interaction give and get clues and hints about their group membership, attitudes, and background knowledge. Much of this exchange of social data occurs through talk: not just what we say, but how we say it. Furthermore, much joking focuses on our ways of speaking, not just our regionally and socially determined habits of pronunciation, word choice, and phrasing, but our slips and logical lapses as well. So joking often has metalingual focus in the sense of Jakobson. And the metalingual dimension of our phrase "Look what the cat drug in" might include signaling the acceptability of traditional folksy sayings or, with appropriate intonation of *drug,* poking fun at nonstandard verb forms.

This covers all but the referential and poetic focuses of Jakobson, both of which might be seen in the joking performance to some degree, though I do not cast that discussion in those terms. Neither focus is particularly relevant for understanding the conversational functions of joking. The referential focus seems to disappear entirely in wordplay, where only the form counts—so the poetic focus on the message itself looms large. As Freud (1905:119) writes, "In one group of these jokes (play upon words) the technique consisted in focussing our psychical attitude upon the *sound* of the word instead of upon its *meaning*—in making the (acoustic) word-presentation itself take the place of its significance as given by its relations to thing-presentations." This passage shows striking parallels with Jakobson's own treatment of the poetic function of language (1960:358): "The poetic function projects the principle of equivalence from the axis of selection onto the axis of combination. Equivalence is promoted to the constitutive device of the sequence. In poetry one syllable is equalized with any other syllable of the sequence." But while our wordplay shows poetic focus in its attention to the form of the message itself, it more obviously realizes metalingual function in commenting on our ways of speaking. The poetics of the narrative joke or anecdote are fascinating in themselves, but not germane to the present study.

The referential function of talk in humorous narratives parallels that in any other narrative text: The listener is justified in expecting personal anecdotes to be true stories, though some stretching for humorous effect may be allowed; but canned narrative jokes represent what Raskin (1985) calls non-bona-fide communication, which means the listener must be prepared to make a "willing suspension of disbelief"—in Coleridge's phrase. The referential status of the joke as a special genre of oral literature and its relation to the standard assumption of mutual cooperation in conversation as discussed by Yamaguchi (1988) are questions tangential to the scope of this study. For present purposes, the progress of conversation leading to the telling of a joke or a personal anecdote, their respective internal organizations, and the differential responses they elicit are central concerns, and these matters receive extended attention in the chapter on organizational aspects of joking and that on joke telling.

Organization

With this background on my functional categories for joking in conversation, we can outline the remainder of this book.

The following three chapters are structured around the functions identified in the foregoing section. Chapter 2 describes the role of joking in the organization of conversation, as well as the internal organization of joking interactions. In chapter 3, I discuss the interpersonal dimension of joking, while chapter 4 narrows the focus to the metalingual function of joking as such.

Chapter 5 concentrates on the narrative forms of humor, jokes and anecdotes, which receive repeated but only cursory attention in the preceding chapters.

Finally, chapter 6 wraps up the findings of this investigation, spells out its conclusions, and suggests directions for future research.

A bibliographical essay on past research relating to conversational joking follows the main text. It covers relevant literature on humor in social interaction, on customary joking relationships, and on psychological aspects of joking and laughter, as well as reviewing linguistic approaches to humor in interaction, and work in Conversation Analysis on joking and laughing.

2

Joking in Conversational Organization

Silence is the unbearable repartee.
G. K. Chesterton, *Charles Dickens* ■

Humor influences the organization of conversation on all levels. Saying "That reminds me of a joke" sets the stage for a performance by one speaker, while the others act as audience. Joking helps us negotiate greetings, fill uncomfortable silences, and change topics without offending anyone. So humor greases the gears of everyday talk and keeps our interactions working smoothly. At the same time, however, overstatement misrepresents the literal facts and a pun may disrupt the customary connection between the two halves of a question-answer sequence. Thus humor may also distract us from the normal business of conversation and urge us into play. Moreover, for some conversationalists, the play portion of any talk may remain quite high even during business transactions. Due either to an individual joking style of conversation or to a habit of joking with certain friends or colleagues, some speakers treat much of their talk as an ongoing competition to out-joke the other participants or at least a certain group of them.

In this chapter, I describe aspects of the interaction between joking and conversational organization, beginning at the micro-level of the utterance pair and working up to higher levels of organization such as openings, closings, topic changes, and the realignment of participants. We shall even see how joking itself can become the primary organizational principle in conversation, when participants engage in punning and banter or when the telling of funny stories turns a conversation into a joke-telling session.

From One Turn to the Next

Spontaneous joking in the form of puns, witty turns of phrase, and sarcasm occurs frequently in everyday conversation, and it can intrude into the organization of our talk at the very level where one utterance hooks up to the next. If we follow Sacks, Schegloff, Jefferson, and other work in Conversation Analysis, then everyday talk in interaction consists of turns taken more or less in rotation by two or more speakers. Further, these turns are organized into so-called adjacency pairs at the micro-level of analysis. An adjacency pair consists of two successive turns such as a question and an answer. The question counts as a "first pair part" which constrains the sort of turn which can occur in the next conversational slot as its "second pair part": In particular, the turn following a question ought to provide an answer to that question, which then counts as the second pair part and completes the adjacency pair.

Now, as Schegloff (1987) points out, the recipient of any utterance which ordinarily requires a response, in particular the first part of an adjacency pair, may choose to "joke first" before producing the relevant second part. In doing a joke-first the recipient of an utterance generally pretends misunderstanding and reanalyzes it in such a way as to clash with the current context. The joke-first often plays on an ambiguity or vagueness in a particular word or phrase, and hence depends not only on a particular semantic content but also on a particular lexical form, as in the punning response below, where the second speaker pretends misunderstanding of *come* as it relates to the current topic of departing in order to suggest a sexual meaning.

A: I'm leaving now. Are you coming?
B: No, just breathing hard.

Once the pretended misunderstanding is recognized as a joke and prompts a small laugh, its speaker usually returns to the serious mode and gives an appropriate response. We may reverse the strategy and pretend to misunderstand an attempted joke-first, treating it as a legitimate misinterpretation and thus refusing to accept the response as a joke at all. The essentially everpresent potential for such joke-firsts has broad consequences for sequentiality in conversation. The first part–second part structure of adjacency pairs looms large in the organization of conversation; add to it the possibility that any second part can be a joking response, and the effects on this basic level of conversational organization can be far-reaching.

The associated sort of role-play, in which a conversationalist pretends to have misunderstood an utterance in order to produce a skewed response to a reanalyzed version of it, provides the basis for spontaneous punning, as we see in the next example. The excerpt comes from four and a half hours of recordings made during the course of an evening which Jason, his wife, Margaret, and their three children spent at the home of Trudy, Roger, and their two children. Jason and Roger are having snacks and drinks in the den before dinner, while the others are scattered throughout the rest of the house. Roger is talking about dolphins within an extended discussion of human intelligence, when Jason creates a pun by reanalyzing the foregoing utterance: He picks up the invented word *poddy* from the previous turn, pretending to take it as a dialect pronunciation of *party,* and cleverly combines it with *animal* in reference to the dolphins being discussed to echo the popular phrase *party animal.*

ROGER: And it seems to be a completely egalitarian *band.*
         There isn't a leader in a dolphin—do they have pods?
JASON: I don't know what they're called.
ROGER: Whales are pods. I don't know what dolphins are. I
         guess they're *pods* too. *Pod*dies. (1.3) Anyway heh
         heh. Yeah but I mean—

JASON::   They're poddy animals.
ROGER: Dheh huh huh.
JASON: Heh heh heh heh *heh* ha ha ha ha ha ha ha ha.
ROGER: Oooh. That's—that's like a blow to the midriff, y'know. Huh huh *huh* huh huh.
JASON: Ha ha *ha* ha ha ha ha ha ha.

This passage not only illustrates spontaneous punning, but also points up the potential of joking to change a topic and to influence the direction of conversation, in this particular case to transform an impending monologue into a more balanced conversation, and so to move from information exchange to group rapport as the goal of the talk exchange.

The appropriate initial response to a pun is, of course, laughter. Thus we can say that joking and laughter are linked as two parts of an adjacency pair as well. As Sacks (1974) points out for narrative jokes, laughter is expected immediately upon completion of the punch line. A failure to laugh at the correct juncture suggests a lack of understanding—or, under the right circumstances, a lack of amusement. Precisely because laughter is expected, silence counts as something missing in the turn-taking pattern; but this silence ambiguously signals either a failure on the part of the audience for not getting the joke or a failure on the part of the teller for a poor performance. The same holds true for spontaneous conversational humor. Since laughter provides the appropriate response to any sort of joking, a lack of laughter suggests the audience either did not get or did not like the joke. Once the audience has laughed, the joker may join in, which makes a further slot available to another participant to make an evaluative comment of the sort Roger produces in the preceding example.

As Sherzer (1978) points out, punning disrupts the ongoing interaction: This pun introduces a frame shift which suggests a topic change and threatens to broaden Roger's monologue into a general play frame. Instead of continuing his speculations on dolphins, Roger feels compelled to comment on Jason's pun: He takes the traditional tack of suggesting how bad the pun was, claiming hyperbolically that it caused him physical pain. This overstatement is met in turn with laughter, which further illustrates the potential of joking to affect the course of a conversation. Moreover, according to the analyses of joking by Sacks (1974) and Sherzer (1985), Jason, in punning, challenges his hearer to get the joke; he poses a test for Roger to pass, which itself amounts to aggression against Roger and a consequent momentary realignment of the two conversationalists. This complex of effects is typical of conversational joking, which can simultaneously instantiate a range of interactional strategies with consequences for the organization of the conversation, both at the immediate micro-level and more globally for the participants and their relations generally.

Further, this same strategy of punning via pretended misunderstanding apparently extends to all participants in a conversation, whether they are directly responding to the first part of an adjacency pair or not. The next passage involves the recently married couple Vera and Jim, at the home of Pamela and Teddy for dinner. Vera is carrying on a conversation with Pamela, which Jim and Teddy have not been involved in up to that point, when Teddy inserts a punning remark just after a comment which places no special restrictions on the next turn.

> VERA: I thought I'd get to see more of him once we got married.
> PAMELA: He he he he.
> TEDDY: But there *was*n't any more of him.
> JIM: Ha ha hehehe.
> VERA: Hehe there wasn't any more of him. Okay. Bum bi bumbum, *cha.*

Teddy brings out an unexpected interpretation for the idiomatic phrase of *see more of someone,* pretending to have understood *more* in reference to physical quantity. Vera repeats the line to show her appreciation, then closes the interchange with an imitation of a drum riff ending in a rim-shot. Teddy's humorous intrusion not only disrupts the prevailing turn-taking structure, and realigns the participants to include him, but also changes the topic. Thus conversationalists may create spontaneous puns constructed around intentional misunderstanding of the foregoing turn, either according to Schegloff's joke-first strategy, producing a nonserious second pair part in response to a serious first part, or by simply intruding an utterance which comments on a reinterpreted prior turn. Either way, the pun can realize interactional aggression in disrupting topical turn-by-turn talk. Since puns are tied into the sequentiality of turn-taking pairs, they can have a wide range of effects on the organization of the conversation in progress. This differentiates punning based on intentional misunderstanding of previous talk from other strategies such as irony, overstatement, and sarcasm for the creation of conversational joking.

A class of stock witticisms built around the very structure of the adjacency pair consists of questions which we use in response to other questions we deem too obvious to deserve a serious reply. Everyone has personal favorites in this class, but the classics "Is the Pope Catholic?" and "Does a bear shit in the woods?" can stand for the group as a whole. These stock phrases respond to a relatively superfluous question with an absolutely superfluous one; they not only fail to provide an answer to the first question, but they also refuse to even conform to the pattern for a proper response as the second part of the adjacency pair. So they doubly violate the requirement that conversational contributions should be relevant (and hence flout Grice's 1975 maxim of relation), which signals to the first speaker that something more is intended. The first speaker must then figure out that the response mirrors the original question, and hence that it was self-evident.

Organizing Larger Chunks of Conversation

Moving now to joking oriented toward conversational chunks larger than the single turn and adjacency pair, we find humorous ways of greeting, taking leave, bridging uncomfortable pauses, or closing down one topic and effecting the transition to another. We can profitably begin this discussion with a consideration of stock, recycled forms for use in such recurrent conversational situations. As we might expect, conversationalists store a wide array of such forms, and some are jocular. So instead of initiating a conversation with a simple and humorless "Hello," we may choose from a repository of standard formulas such as "Look what the cat drug in" or "We can't go on meeting like this" under appropriate circumstances. There is a special proverbial formula for heralding the sudden appearance of a person who has been the topic of our talk, namely "Speak of the devil, and he will appear," from which we often cite only the introductory four-word phrase, sometimes as "Speaking of the devil"; and this formula naturally provides a humorous strategy for integrating a new arrival into a conversation, when applied in a technically infelicitious way to someone not under discussion.

Similarly, in taking leave, we may pass over the uncolored "goodbye" and "bye-bye" in favor of jocular stock phrases like "See you in the funny papers" and "Don't take any wooden nickels." In fact, many speakers seem to follow what we might call a "leave-'em-laughing" strategy, according to which they always try to conclude an interaction with a line which leaves their interlocutor laughing as they depart. So it is only natural to find not just stock jocular leave-taking phrases like those above, but also stock responses to serious goodbyes, as the following pairs illustrate:

(1) A: See you.
    B: Not if I see you first.

(2) A: See you later.
    B: Yeah, *much* later.

(3) A: Take it easy.
    B: Yeah, but take it.

Of course, if both or all participants in a conversation adhere to this leave-'em-laughing strategy, a competitive situation must arise at the closing, as each person hopes to land a funny line, then depart before anyone else can produce a counter-joke. This competition fits in with the "ritual combat" strategy which Tannen (1990) identifies as characteristic of talk interactions between males, and it represents one facet of what I have been calling a customary joking relationship; it is presumably responsible for the classic pair below, consisting of a second stock jocular response to what was already a jocular leave-taking formula.

A: See you later, alligator.
B: After while, crocodile.

Besides these formulas for greetings, welcomings, and closings, conversationalists store and recycle humorous phrases tailored to bridge an uncomfortable pause or to wrap up an old topic and to segue into a new one. A proverbial phrase for prompting a silent co-conversationalist who seems unable or unwilling to produce a response to the first part of an adjacency pair is *Cat got your tongue?* To fill an overlong pause in a group conversation, many speakers also use the traditional phrase *Quaker meeting,* for some associated with the introduction to a children's game, *Quaker meeting has begun.* . . . Current lines in the category of phrases for the transition from one topic to another may have originated in or been popularized by television, for instance, *Moving right along* and *Meanwhile, back at the ranch.* We have special formulas for effecting the transition from a joke or period of nonserious talk into a new topic, namely, *But seriously, folks* and *But all kidding aside.* The latter finds its stock ironic counterpart in *But all seriousness aside,* which creates additional mirth as often as it actually transitions into serious talk, so it might with equal justification classify as a stock witticism with a narrowly defined conversational slot.

Spontaneous joking, of course, also occurs at crucial points in conversation: to break the ice in openings and in welcoming new participants, to close down an old topic and move into a new one, or to wind down the conversation and take leave. The next excerpt shows spontaneous joking in a greeting exchange. This passage comes from the beginning of the recorded evening mentioned above which Margaret, Jason, and children spent at the home of Trudy, Roger, and children. Jason is arriving somewhat later than the rest of his family. He enters with a sarcastic line about the holidays, now two weeks past, as he hands over to Roger a bottle decorated with holly and red ribbon. Jason's son, David, and the hostess, Trudy, both address him jocularly as *snowman,* since he is covered with a sprinkling of snow from his walk over. Trudy says *How cute* of a tam she sees Jason wearing for the first time, while Roger prefers to comment sarcastically on the new headgear by asking Jason whether it is *Scottish night.*

MARGARET:	Oh there's Jason. See *he* comes to the *front* door.
ROGER:	Sure. (2.0) Jason sensibly came to the *front* door. (5.0) {opening door} Hey. (3.0) Welcome welcome.
JASON:	Happy holiday festivities.
DAVID:	Hi snowman hehhehheh.
TRUDY:	Hi snowman hheh.
ROGER:	Heh heh heh heh heh. Is this uh
JASON:	Did Margaret bring my
TRUDY:	How *cute.*
ROGER:	Scottish night? Heh heh heh.
JASON:	Bring my uh
TRUDY:	Okay. I have to admit. Um,
ROGER:	Margaret has a . . .

This whole interchange then thrives on attempts to make others laugh. And this is hardly atypical of greeting and leave-taking exchanges generally. When spontaneous joking comes thick and fast, as it does here, laughter apparently becomes appropriate at any juncture, so that we are hard put to say exactly what any participant is laughing about, for instance whether Roger laughs in response to Jason's sarcasm, David and Trudy's intentionally misapplied appellation *snowman,* or both.

The next passage again illustrates joking surrounding the introduction of a newly arrived guest, but this time it is a mutual acquaintance, Andy, who just happened to drop by the home of Teddy and Pamela during the dinner with their invited guests, Vera and Jim, mentioned above. Vera and Jim answer the door, since Teddy and Pamela are occupied with dinner preparations. Vera initiates a humorous *key*—in the sense of Hymes (1972)— for the interaction with her overstated stress on *still* and *four,* sarcastically suggesting that marriage has perhaps not been all she thought it might be, as she glances roguishly around toward her husband, Jim.

VERA: Hi.
ANDY: You don't remember me.
VERA: Yes I *do*. Yes I *do*.
ANDY: I haven't seen you since you were married.
VERA: That's true. And we're *still* married. It's been *four* months.
TEDDY: {arriving} It's not a record *yet,* but it's y'know.
VERA: He he.
ANDY: Huh huh huh.
JIM: It's a record for *me*.
VERA: Yeah [he he.]
TEDDY: [Ha ha] ha heh heh. It's starting to *feel* like a record.
VERA: He *ha* ha ha ha ha ha.
TEDDY: Huh he he.

Once Vera establishes the humorous tone, Teddy picks up her lead with a sarcastic comment about the four-month duration of the marriage as establishing a record. Both Vera and Andy in turn respond appropriately with laughter, while Jim moves on into a joke of his own based on the idea that the marriage is setting longevity records. Vera agrees to his comment with *Yeah* and laughs, while Teddy laughs and then further builds on Jim's line with another attempt at humor, thus finally running the joke into the ground. The passage illustrates not only how conversationalists use joking to negotiate the introduction of a new arrival, but also how they weave together humorous variations on a theme, each building on foregoing utterances to contribute their own facetious comments.

Banter and Mocking

This rapid exchange of humorous lines oriented toward a common theme, though aimed primarily at mutual entertainment rather than topical talk, typifies what we generally call "banter."

In the passage above it consists only of sarcastic comments, rather than wordplay in the usual sense of punning, extended metaphor, and so on, but it may contain either or both mixed. No matter what else a set of conversationalists are involved in, whether they are greeting a new arrival as above, mocking someone for an alleged logical lapse as in the next excerpt, or whatever, banter seems to occur with this sort of structure.

In the passage below, the banter takes the form of wordplay in the strict sense. It occurs between two brothers, Brandon and Ned, who are laughing about what they consider an illogical remark by their mother, Lydia, overheard from the adjoining room, where Lydia is talking to Brandon's daughter. Visiting at the home of their parents, Brandon and Ned fall back into patterns of talk developed when they were young: They laugh about their mother's habits of unreflected speech and at each other's verbal slips, as well as engaging in wordplay freely.

> LYDIA: We had such a nice day today, so you hurry and get rested. Because you're gonna have a big nice [day tomorrow.]
> BRANDON: [Hurry and get] rested.
> NED: Uhhuhhuhhuhhuhhuh hehe.
> BRANDON: That's oxymoronic.
> NED: Uhhuhhuhhuh. Yeah. Can you imagine the ox? Hehehe
> BRANDON: No. But I've spotted the moron.
> NED: I see. Huhhuhhuh. You'd think as dumb as oxes are. To call one a moron would be tautological. Huhhahaheh.

Notice first that Brandon overlaps with the end of Lydia's sentence, but it does not count as a real interruption, since Lydia cannot hear it in the next room, and the others have not been attending to what she is saying anyway. Once Ned shows his appreciation with laughter, Brandon goes on to comment precisely on the nature of Lydia's infelicitous utterance. This comment sets off some complex verbal fireworks, which shows how wordplay itself may become the primary cohesive element in a conversation. Ned begins to reanalyze *oxymoron* into its folk-etymological elements with *Can you imagine the ox?;* then Brandon takes over with a new suggestion: *I've spotted the moron.* Finally, Ned draws the proposed *ox* and *moron* segments together and rounds out the whole exchange with a reference to tautology, which resonates with the original meaning of *oxymoron.* Punning ceases to count as disruptive in the sense of Sherzer (1978) when the goal of conversation itself consists in wordplay, rather than in the exchange of information and narratives. If we engage in conversation to enhance rapport and pass the time of day pleasantly, then punning may amount to the cohesive force in a stretch of conversation.

It is worthy of comment that Ned freely laughs at Brandon's lines and even at his own, while Brandon produces no audible sign of amusement, though he is clearly involved in the wordplay and enjoying himself. This particular posture represents Brandon's individual joking style. Brandon follows a competitive strategy in which conversational joking is a game to be won or lost. Ned, by contrast, seems to view joking as a cooperative activity accruing to mutual entertainment with everyone a winner. Perhaps predictably, both Ned and Brandon himself consider Brandon the superior performer and conversational humorist.

But what we see here from the perspective of conversational organization at issue is that Brandon initiates a realignment of the participants. In commenting on the alleged oxymoron, Brandon opens a side conversation in which he and Ned align themselves against Lydia. They conspire together to poke fun at her previous turn, and to exclude her from their developing conversation, because they feel she fails to meet their logical standards for talk.

Beyond their function of realigning the potential participants in a conversation, Brandon's mocking repeat and comment deserve our attention due to their metalingual thrust, in the sense of Jakobson (1960), and the punning they elicit. We see here the metalingual function of joking in commenting on the form of talk, and its social or group control function of labeling some sorts of talk as inappropriate within the ongoing interaction. Significantly, Brandon and Ned share the joke and the metalingual comment on Lydia's seemingly contradictory speech, but Lydia herself receives no feedback from them in this instance. The metalingual force of conversational joking deserves extensive comment, and it makes up the central subject matter of a separate chapter below.

By way of comparison, let us look at an excerpt in which one speaker makes a sarcastic comment directly to a preceding speaker for saying something silly. In it, Amy mocks her mother, Patricia, for saying she would have made the toasted cheese sandwiches better if she had known Fred was staying for supper; but Amy waits until Fred has completed the apology-acceptance sequence before speaking. Amy and Mary are undergraduate students who have returned to the home of their mother and father, Patricia and Ralph, for the long Thanksgiving weekend. Amy's boyfriend, Fred, spends a lot of time with her family when she is home, and he has been invited for supper this evening, which Mary was recording.

> PATRICIA: Fred. I really didn't expect you tonight. I'd have made this better if I'd have known you were coming, but.
> FRED: (h)Tha(ha)t's (h)all [(h)ri(hi)ght hehe.]
> AMY: [You'd have made] gour*met* grilled cheese.
> FRED: Ah he he ha ha ha [ha ha.]
> RALPH: [Huh huh] huh huh huhhuh.
> PATRICIA: [Hehheh]
>   hehhehhehhehhehheh. (h)I love heh heh I love it.
> MARY: Gourmet grilled cheese.

Interactionally, Amy aligns herself with Fred, and against her mother, Patricia, for pretending she can really do anything special with grilled cheese sandwiches. She pokes fun at Patricia's pretense with the hyperbolic *gourmet grilled cheese,* as if grilled cheese could serve as the basis for a gourmet food. The form *You'd have made* more directly places the phrase in Patricia's mouth than *She'd have made:* With it, Amy exacerbates Patricia's original claim by extrapolating from it one which sounds more obviously incongruous. From the standpoint of conversational organization, Amy not only realigns the participants, she also opens up the conversation for everyone present and introduces a humorous key for the coming interaction. But Patricia refuses to act like the butt of the joke: She not only laughs as much as everyone else, but also comments positively on the jest with *I love it.* Once Fred and Ralph have laughed, Patricia might at least have withheld approval with silence or, better, have countered with a comment or joke of her own. Instead, she rolls with the punch, enjoys the humor, and even compliments the daughter who mocked her. So Patricia seems also to follow the strategy we saw Ned employ above, namely enjoying the jokes as they come without concern for some sort of score keeping in a competitive game. Mary's repetition of *gourmet grilled cheese* once the laughter has died down represents a savoring of the line and fixes it as a kind of formula, which recurs several more times in attempts at humor later in the conversation.

Finally, I would like to consider a passage from a two-party conversation in which one participant directly mocks the other for an infelicitous formulation. This situation differs from the foregoing ones, in that the single listener himself serves as the butt of the joke. In an excerpt like this, where a second-speaker repeat identifies a whole stretch of speech as in need of correction, the first speaker must deal not only with the challenge of discovering and resolving the problem but also with the embarrassment of having made an error. This passage again involves talk between the two brothers, Brandon and Ned, introduced in a preceding episode; Brandon is attempting to justify the didactic tendency Ned has objected to in some of director Frank Capra's later films.

BRANDON:	A lot of what he was after in some of these films, was this concern about America. And what was going on in the world, and about the little guy, and the de*press*ion, and-
NED:	I understand that.
BRANDON:	Y'know.
NED:	I'm in favor of the depression. I think you can [do that-]
BRANDON:	[Haha] (h)I'm in *fav*or of the de*press*ion [hahahehehe.]
NED:	[Hhaw.] I'm in favor of the little guy, especially in times *like* the depression.

Nevertheless, even in challenging or testing Ned—as Sacks and Sherzer would have it—Brandon gives him sufficient reconstruction of the blunder for easy recognition; and in spite of potential embarrassment and the test posed in having to find and correct the error, Ned is laughing about his own slip even as he produces his clarification.

Notice, furthermore, that Brandon repeats the slip word-for-word, including the first person pronoun *I,* instead of switching to *you.* It initially seems odd that he chooses not to make the regular deictic pronoun shift. By retaining *I,* however, Brandon makes it perfectly clear that his repeat serves only to identify the locus of an error in form, rather than to challenge Ned for the content of the utterance: He signals his recognition that this is a pure slip of the tongue, which Ned will correct immediately once he is made aware of it. *You're in favor of the depression,* by contrast, implies that Ned actually holds the opinion expressed, so it presents a more serious challenge. A response like *So you approve of the depression, do you?* takes the challenge even further, first by going beyond repeating Ned's words to ascribing beliefs to him, and second by making recovery of the original slip more difficult. Such a move seems to occupy a middle ground between local repetition and the intertextual reconstruction of previous talk, which Tannen (1989) discusses.

In fact, there is a potential three-way contrast even within the realm of pure repetition, since Brandon could say *He's in favor of the depression.* In the presence of other hearers, this would amount to Brandon's aligning himself against Ned, making him feel compelled to defend his view or at least explain the blunder; but even in the absence of a real audience, a second speaker could use the third-person pronoun in a repeat like this as if to identify an error for imagined hearers, and thus to take sides with them. So Brandon really chooses the least threatening of various parallel forms for his turn, and the exchange as a whole conduces more to bonding between the two participants than to face loss or gain for either one. And in general among approximate social equals, joking usually serves to defuse aggression and create solidarity. Hence spontaneous joking ends up more a matter of group cohesion than testing; and even the testing serves as a control on what sorts of talk are acceptable to participants in the interaction.

The Organization of Joke Telling

I turn now to a brief consideration of joke telling, in particular, in keeping with the goal of this chapter, as it affects conversational organization; the internal organization of the joke performance along with the role of the audience in it are complex phenomena in their own right, and they receive extended attention in chapter 5. The relevance joke telling has for the organization of conversation becomes obvious whenever one participant announces the performance of a joke with some phrase like "Stop me if you've heard this one." If the other conversationalists offer encouragement—and sometimes even in spite of their attempts to interrupt the telling—the first speaker goes on to perform a joke recalled from some earlier conversation for an audience consisting of the other participants.

Any number of stock phrases such as "That reminds me of a joke" or "I've got a joke for you" seek to justify an interruption of the current topic of conversation. These phrases introduce the *preface* to a joke-telling, according to Sacks (1974), and they routinely herald some characterization of the joke as well, so that the audience can decide whether they know it or not. Such an introduction calls for some response by another participant. This response may stop the joke-telling, if the other participants are familiar with the joke announced. But once the others agree to the telling, the original speaker lays claim to the floor for an indeterminate number of turns, and the audience has a right to expect something in the way of entertainment. The joke-teller then commands a disproportionate share of speaking time, but is simultaneously committed thereby to performing for the others. This constitutes a radical realignment of participants with more or less equal access to the floor under normal conditions. So the telling of a recalled, recycled joke sets up a performer-audience dichotomy with a somewhat different dynamic than that found in punning and banter where each participant tries to contribute something funny in turn.

Sacks (1974) provided the first careful examination of the course of a joke's telling in conversation. He showed that it follows the pattern for story telling generally; the major difference consists in the expected response of laughter for the joke. Sacks illustrates the finely tuned organization of the teller's performance and the audience response at a precise point following the punch line. As he points out, the expectation of laughter at the close of a joke makes its absence significant as a sign either of disapproval or of a failure to understand. Production of mirthless laughter at the proper juncture thus serves the dual purpose of demonstrating understanding *and* a lack of appreciation. I turn shortly to the function of laughter in the organization of conversation as a topic in its own right. But we should observe at this point that the interactional view of conversational humor presented in this study downplays the test function of jokes and joking in everyday conversation among adults. Accordingly, the test function of joke telling recedes behind its character as performance and entertainment, so that the precise timing of laughter assumes less importance, and telling a joke becomes more like telling any other story.

As to the positioning of jokes in conversation, participants can tell a joke at almost any point after the opening and before the pre-closing sections, as described by Schegloff (1968) and Schegloff and Sacks (1973); nevertheless, they generally introduce them when they become topically relevant or once spontaneous joking has already established a play frame in the sense of Fry (1963). Then, apparently, telling one joke makes the telling of any other joke topically relevant, though participants do tend to follow a joke with another on a related topic or of the same structural type, so that one dirty joke suggests another and, alas, one ethnic riddle joke conforming to the pattern below leads to another as well.

QUESTION: How many Poles/WASPs/Italians does it take to accomplish some (usually simple) task?

ANSWER: Some number (usually larger than expected): Some smaller number to do one part of the task, the remainder to finish it.

Consequently, conversationalists often end up telling jokes in rounds or joke-telling sessions, in which humor as performance and entertainment becomes the primary organizational factor in the interaction. These sessions frequently assume the character of a competition in which each succeeding teller tries to outdo the former one.

Nevertheless, the telling of a joke may also naturally lead into discussion of its topic or other serious matters. Hence, even in joking sessions, one often encounters serious, topical talk between the jokes. The dirty joke that Sacks (1974) analyzes raises a number of questions about sex for its adolescent audience, so it naturally prompts them to ask the teller just what he knows about the scenes the joke describes. Again, in an extended passage cited in chapter 5 below, we shall see how a series of three related jokes naturally segues into a discussion of what constitutes a dirty joke. Thus joke telling takes place within the normal flow of topics in a conversation.

Laughter in Conversational Organization

As we have seen in the foregoing discussion, laughter represents the appropriate response to both narrative jokes and spontaneous conversational joking in the form of puns, sarcasm, irony, and so on. Given that laughter shows amusement, a conversationalist may produce laughter in response to the previous utterance to point out something funny about it, as Schenkein (1972) and Jefferson (1979) have shown. Thus in the excerpt below Jim laughs heartily at Teddy's apparent tautology, which leads Teddy to join in the laughter and comment disparagingly about his own alleged logical lapse. Jim repeats his laughter at the end to close the sequence. This excerpt stems from the same evening of recording mentioned above, in which Jim and Vera have been invited for dinner at the home of Pamela and Teddy. After dinner the two couples are talking about how children grow up and learn: Teddy is describing how his daughter, Sara, has put off his attempts to get her to read.

> TEDDY: And I say to her, Sara if you could read now. For yourself. *You* could read.

JIM: Uh ha ha *ba* hahaha. Ha*ba*ha.
TEDDY: Uhhuh. Which I suppose is almost too obvious even
       to tell a five-year-old.
JIM: Huh huh huh huh huh huh.

In parallel fashion, again following Schenkein and Jefferson, conversationalists may intersperse laughter in their own utterances
in order to signal amusement and invite laughter from other
participants. It is generally considered rather bad form for the
teller of a joke to initiate laughter at its punch line; but once the
audience has begun to laugh, the teller may join in as well. By
contrast, no stigma adheres to laughing during the course of a
story, say to show amusement at the scene depicted, at some
silly character, or the like. For instance, in the following passage,
Roslyn starts to laugh during her short narrative as she pro-
nounces *seance,* perhaps to signal a nonserious stance toward
the event or embarrassment at having been a party to it. Either
way, her laughter has the effect of getting Nancy to laugh along
with her. Roslyn is an old friend enjoying a farewell dinner with
Nancy before leaving the area for a new position.

ROSLYN: There was this girl I grew up with. She came to my
          house only once. And we were sitting under the table
          having a sea(haha)nce he[hehe.]
NANCY: [Haha] ha ha.
ROSLYN: She never came ba(ha)ck huh huh.

Of course, if laughter regularly accompanies a nonserious stance
toward reported incidents and, hence, a psychological distance
from our own past activities, then it seems conversationalists
might also expropriate laughter as a device for signaling a re-
sistence to taking some matter too seriously, and this is just what
Jefferson (1984a, 1984b) finds in talk about troubles.

   Jefferson shows how speaker laughter in troubles talk works
to defuse seriousness, though it does not invite hearer laughter,
and hearers respond seriously, usually with expressions of consolation or agreement as in the passage below. Here Sally and
Leona are secretaries in a university office. They have agreed to
having their talk recorded by a graduate assistant, Tamara, who

is present but not verbally involved in this particular segment of conversation.

SALLY: It's the little things, y'know?
LEONA: Yeah. And those little things always happen here heh heh heh
SALLY: But he does that a lot.

This sort of laughter reduces the threat posed by the teller's troubles for the hearer. It shows the speaker is coping with her troubles; and the supportive response from the hearer shows she takes the problem seriously. Once consolation has been expressed, the stage is set for entry into closing or transition to an unrelated topic.

The routine conversational association of laughter with psychological distance from the events described further makes laughter available to signal embarrassment in talk about our own behavior. In the example before last, Roslyn laughed about a seance she once participated in, which signaled a nonserious stance toward the event and, hence, potential embarrassment about it from her current perspective. Laughter in this context shows the speaker feels embarrassed but hopes the hearer will understand; the hearer may join in the laughter to indicate that she finds the event humorous rather than shameful—which would be inappropriate in the foregoing case—or pause and move on to another topic to avoid further embarrassment for the first speaker. Jefferson, Sacks, and Schegloff (1976) discuss this among other consequences of laughing together. We see this latter strategy at work in the next excerpt, where, apparently to show embarrassment, Sandra intersperses laughter in a sort of confession during talk about paying bills. Sandra and Greg are undergraduate students engaged to be married: This portion of Sandra's extensive recording took place in Greg's car in the parking lot of a drive-in restaurant.

GREG: It's enough to get some initial bills paid. And it'll take care of my heat, and the electricity and the *phone.*
        (2.5)

SANDRA: Huh huh Mine won't even cover huh huh my Sears
          credit card. I can't wait for that bill.
          (4.5)
  GREG: But I know I've got- I was calculating how much I
          was going to get . . .

Greg responds with initial silence and a subsequent topic shift.
This again points up the function of laughter, and particularly
embarrassed laughter, in closing down a topic.

Though further talk may be rather long in coming, as the next
passage shows, interlocutors do not express sympathy, since this
would be tantamount to judging the minor embarrassment a
major problem. In this passage, Sandra is at the home of her
parents talking to her aunt and uncle, Ruth and Harry, about her
drive from the university.

HARRY: How many miles *is* it?
 RUTH: From here to,
SANDRA: It takes two hours. If we made a direct route, it
         would only take about an hour uh huh huh huh.
         (0.5) {inhales} I think. It wouldn't take us two hours,
         but,
 RUTH: But your uh *cou*sins don't go there now?

These examples illustrate something close to so-called nervous
laughter. Both embarrassed laughter and nervous laughter signal
discomfort with the current topic; they seek not to elicit hearer
laughter in response, but rather to close the current topic down
and to move into another topic or a closing sequence.

This makes four different sorts of laughter all associated with
the end of a chunk of conversation. First, laughter is the appropriate response at the end of a narrative joke. Second, as Jefferson
describes, laughter regularly occurs in troubles talk to defuse
seriousness, where it elicits consolation and closure. Third, laughter in an embarrassed confession of a silly habit or event related
to the topic of talk also serves as a move toward closure. And,
fourth, nervous laughter signals discomfort with the current
topic, and thus initiates a closing sequence as well. Consequently,
as Schenkein (1972:366) notes, laughter by itself comes to signal

the ends of topics and conversations; it acts as a "discourse marker," in the sense of Schiffrin (1987), for signaling closure.

My final excerpt for this chapter takes us back to the recording cited above where two secretaries and a student assistant are conversing in an office, though only Leona and the student, Tamara, actually talk in this passage. Tamara has jocularly reported to the others a warning she heard to beware of women who wear makeup. Then she goes on to say she has encouraged a certain man to talk to her: Since she wears no makeup, he should have no cause for worry. This elicits two questions from Leona, more to signal disbelief than desire for confirmation. Thus Tamara gives only a short laugh by way of response to Leona; and this leads Leona to comment and laugh about Tamara's logic in the next turn. When Tamara laughs again on the heels of laughter by Leona, it effectively closes the whole sequence, so that Leona reverts to the secretarial business at hand after a short pause.

TAMARA:	Right.
LEONA:	Why not? Because you're not wearing makeup?
TAMARA:	Ehheh.
LEONA:	Oh what logic. hehe.
TAMARA:	Heh heh.
	(1.0)
LEONA:	Okay. So. November third. Jerry has not given us a date yet.

We saw this same pattern in the first example cited in this section. There, too, the hearer, Jim, laughs to point out something funny in the foregoing turn, and the first speaker, Teddy, laughs and comments to show he recognizes the joke and takes no offense. When Jim laughs a second time in response to Teddy, it apparently leaves no room for further additions to the sequence.

By way of summary, we have seen how conversationalists may place laughter in certain positions so as to organize their talk. Laughter serves not only to respond to jokes and joking. By virtue of its regular association with hilarity, laughter works more generally as a marker of a nonserious attitude. In response to a serious utterance, laughter can point out its humorous potential to other participants. Within a story or description, the nonserious stance signaled by laughter can indicate not only genuine amusement, but also psychological distance and embarrassment. Then, this association with embarrassment makes laughter available to signal discomfort with a topic or a whole interaction, and hence to move into a closing sequence. The clustering of laugh tokens near the ends of topics and whole conversations makes laughter available as a discourse marker indicating closure.

Conclusions

We have seen how a joke-first practice hits at the very basis of the micro-organization of conversation. This practice is available not only as the second, response part of an adjacency pair, but to anyone who chooses to pretend misunderstanding of the foregoing turn to produce a pun. The joke-first practice results in a range of stock witticisms as responses tailored to recurrent second part slots. These stock witticisms cluster around specific areas of conversation: openings, closings, topic changes, and so on. We also find recurrent functions for spontaneous conversational joking in these same positions, particularly in the realignment of participants, creation of a new side conversation, signaling, and testing for attitudes and membership in groups. Both stock and spontaneous puns can be interactionally aggressive in disrupting topical turn-by-turn talk. We have further seen the need to distinguish, first, the aggression of canned jokes from that of spontaneous joking and, second, within the realm of spontaneous joking, the aggression of wordplay from that of sarcasm directed at a present participant. Conversationalists typically introduce narrative jokes only where topically relevant, though wordplay often naturally leads into joke telling, and the telling of any joke makes any other joke topically relevant. Laughter regularly follows jokes and stories, so it becomes available as a discourse marker to close an uncomfortable topic; laughter also indicates genuine amusement, say at a foregoing error, so it becomes available as an interactional resource to invite attention and laughter to a slip, and to show distance from a problem and resistance to it. Consequently we must recognize a multiplicity of functions for laughter.

3

The Interpersonal Dimension of Conversational Joking

> For friends must be of the same humor and inclina-
> tions too, or else the league of amity, though made
> with ever so many protestations, will soon be broke.
>
> Erasmus, *In Praise of Folly* ■

We have so far begun to get a sense of the role of humor in conversation, of its multiple functions on all levels of organization. We have seen the testing and aggressive aspects of conversational joking. They follow from the fact that a joke calls for laughter immediately upon its completion, which narrowly determines the range of responses the listener can make. But we have also seen how conversationalists use stock and spontaneous humor to negotiate openings, closings, topic changes and realignments, and how they interact in so-called banter to produce extended sequences of wordplay oriented toward some topic. So conversational joking allows participants to perform for their mutual entertainment with a consequent enhancement of rapport. We are developing an interactional perspective in which humor is seen as helping smooth the work in everyday conversation, as well as offering us a chance to play: to present a self, test for common ground, and create rapport in entertaining fashion.

In this chapter, I would like to take a closer look at these interpersonal functions of self-presentation, testing, and rapport-building across a range of joking types. I will begin with personal anecdotes then move into forms of wordplay such as punning, hyperbole, and allusion, then on to mocking and sarcasm—that is, from those apparently harmless forms geared to mutual revelation, to those forms aggressive only in testing for understanding, then on to forms clearly aggressive in attacking the personal characteristics and errors of others. It is easy to claim that swapping funny personal anecdotes allows self-presentation and contributes to rapport directly, whereas competitive wordplay substitutes a show of wit for the presentation of self, while its test function looms large. However, puns may also be seen to enhance rapport indirectly, since passing the tests they pose demonstrates shared knowledge and group membership.

By contrast, sarcastic comments on the foibles and slips of fellow conversationalists not only require less wit and pose simpler tests than puns, but also seem geared to produce animosity rather than rapport, which makes their interpersonal function as a whole problematic. Nevertheless, some conversationalists apparently thrill to the competition and hardly covert aggression of mocking and sarcasm, wordplay and innuendo. In fact, some friends and colleagues develop what I have been calling a customary joking relationship, where joking routinely takes the form of verbal attack, competitive wordplay, teasing, and so on. Goody (1978) and Apte (1985) describe such customary joking relationships by contrast with more highly formalized kinship-based joking relationships found in traditional tribal societies. A customary joking relationship may serve a rapport function between some conversationalists; and this helps explain the apparently positive role of mocking and sarcasm in their talk exchanges.

I hope to show how the interactional perspective on joking being developed here can incorporate current thinking from linguistic pragmatics and discourse analysis on politeness and distance, power and solidarity. This will help us account for the whole range of interpersonal functions realized with the various types of conversational humor. At the same time, I have tried to choose exemplary cases of joking patterns which recur in my extensive data base, so that the progressive analysis of illustrative examples will provide a rough and ready catalogue of the range of conversational joking strategies.

Personal Anecdotes

Everyday conversation thrives on narratives. Tannen (1989) identifies story telling as one of the primary strategies for creating rapport. In exchanging stories about our personal lives, we present a self for ratification by other participants in the conversation and we "gather relevant social data" about these others, in the sense of Goffman (1959). To the extent that we accept the selves presented in the personal narratives we tell each other, we create solidarity and rapport between us. And, of course, many of the narratives we relate are funny. Laughing together further enhances the rapport which develops from sharing personal anecdotes. Morreall (1990) argues that funny stories we tell about ourselves are more efficient tools of humor than canned jokes, first because they grow out of our personal experience, and second because we tailor them to fit the current context. This makes personal anecdotes all the more effective in nurturing rapport. Even a personal anecdote told many times before can arise in and take on the feel of its immediate context, while at the same time reflecting the individual perceptions and feelings of the teller. So the successful performance of a funny personal story can help the teller present a self through talk in many ways at once.

Besides relating authentic personal experiences, conversationalists may recycle a witty story heard elsewhere, presenting it as their own experience. If their listeners already know the story, however, it tends to fall flat. Morreall argues that a borrowed narrative can never come up to a genuine personal one in humor, since it lacks spontaneity and the reality which derives from attachment to a real individual. Thus, in the passage below involving three undergraduate students who work together in the departmental copying room several hours a week, Judy presents a canned humorous narrative as her own experience, and manages to elicit only *aws* and disappointed comment.

> BETH: . . . like a nightmare? You woke up with your arms around you.
>
> JUDY: I've had dreams about eating marshmallows. I woke up and my pillow was gone.
>
> ARNOLD: Aw.
>
> BETH: Aw. *Ju*dy. That's silly.

The scene Judy presents is too farfetched and unrealistic to pass for genuine personal experience, even for listeners unfamiliar with this story, so it yields no amusement and results in a loss of face for Judy. In spite of its trite unfunniness, Judy's little sequence does compactly represent the characteristic narrative structure we will find in the personal anecdote, consisting, as it does, of a topic statement followed by two related clauses with a temporal juncture, in the sense of Labov and Waletzky (1967). And this narrative typically sets up slots for audience response—preferably laughter—and comment.

The range of possible personal anecdotes follows certain guidelines. While conversationalists sometimes relate humorous stories about their own past successes, say landing a particularly apt repartee or having outwitted some more powerful adversary, adult participants in the conversations I reviewed usually avoid such narratives, presumably because they may be heard as more or less sanctioned forms of bragging. Up through adolescence, funny tales in which the speaker puts down an authority figure are fairly well received, but adults are more likely to report on the successes of their family and friends than on their own, and even then they may be faulted for indirectly blowing their own horn. Nor dare they become careless and overdo their telling of stories about high-prestige friends and acquaintances, lest their listeners should accuse them of name-dropping. While any of these forms of self-aggrandizement may gain respect for the teller, they often serve to awaken the competitive urges of other participants as well, which can lead to critical comments and/or story-topping, and hence to loss of face in the longer run.

Perhaps for these reasons, when adults told humorous personal anecdotes in my recorded data they tended toward stories about their own foibles and errors. These stories enlist others on the side of their tellers; they elicit sympathy and solidarity with them rather than competition. We all recall funny events from our childhoods and we engage in embarrassing behavior from time to time, so there is never a dearth of tellable material, nor a lack of understanding. Though teenagers may still feel threatened by their childhood silliness, adults tend to view their earlier errors and excesses as cause for amusement rather than scorn. In fact, funny personal anecdotes end up presenting a positive self-image rather than a negative one. First of all, they convey a so-called sense of humor, which counts as a virtue in our society. They present a self with an ability to laugh at problems and overcome them—again an admirable character trait. So apparently self-effacing personal anecdotes redound to conversational rapport and positive face for the teller in several ways at once.

Much of the functioning and dynamics of personal anecdotes comes out in the serially connected excerpts that follow. The examples again come from a set of six forty-five-minute segments recorded at the home of Pamela and Teddy with their invited dinner guests, Vera and Jim. Vera and Jim are recently married and childless, while Pamela and Teddy have two children. Dinner and dessert are over, the kids are in bed, and the adults are all relating their own childhood memories. When the foursome broke into dyads of two men and two women respectively, Vera overheard Jim mention a letter he wrote to a six-year-old girlfriend, and she asks him about it when she gets a chance, which serves as a preface to the story, in the sense of Sacks (1972) and Jefferson (1978). Then her request *Well tell me about it* aligns her as recipient vis-à-vis Jim as teller. But Jim opts to provide some background information in the form of two related humorous anecdotes about the girl in question. The first illustrates a slight expansion of the minimum anecdote form cited above. It contains an initial scene-setting statement, which immediately elicits laughter; then follow two clauses run together into a single unit with *and*s providing temporal sequencing.

> VERA: Were you talking about *you* having a girlfriend when you were little and writing her this letter.
> JIM: Yeah. Yeah.
> VERA: Well *tell* me about it.
> TEDDY: Uhhhuh.

JIM: As I recall, she and I had matching Superman suits
[and we'd-]
VERA: [Ahhahahahaha]
TEDDY: [Hhuh huh huh]
PAMELA: [Heh heh heh heh heh heh heh]
JIM: and we'd lie on the back lawn
[and pretend to be flying and stuff.]
VERA: [The basis of true love. Yes.]

Jim does not really go much beyond describing a scene from his childhood, but he drawls out the introductory formula *As I recall* to set up a story-telling frame, and he delivers the first line rapidly for maximum effect. When laughter ensues, Jim immediately cuts off his second sentence, then restarts once the laughter dies down. So he plays this little scene for all it is worth.

The laughter following the initial setup for the anecdote differs from that which responds to the punch line of a narrative joke. According to Sacks (1974) and Sherzer (1985), narrative jokes are constructed so as to build up to the final punch line, which imposes an understanding test on the listener. The listener then laughs to demonstrate understanding. But personal anecdotes have no punch line as such, and they do not pose a test. Instead, the anecdote presents an amusing scene which invites listeners to laugh and offer comments of their own. Apparently some events like this image of two kids lying on the lawn in Superman suits automatically elicit laughter if presented properly. Even a simple statement of fact may strike us as quite funny: For instance, in a discussion the other day, about which schools each of several students had attended previously, a University of Texas graduate set off gales of laughter by telling an alumnus of Amherst College that she had attended freshman lectures larger than his whole student body. Although the statement reports a seemingly neutral fact, it entails the same sort of incongruity we find funny in intentional hyperbole. Still, this statement alone would not usually classify as conversational humor, let alone as joking or a personal anecdote.

Jim's wife, Vera, comments sarcastically on the scene depicted before Jim even has a chance to finish. Evaluative comments from listeners, themselves intended to elicit further laughter, routinely appear at the close of a funny anecdote or almost anytime after the initial statement of plot or theme, and quite freely once laughter has interrupted it. This means anecdotes disrupt the flow of conversation less than canned jokes do: They produce almost immediate audience participation, and thus work less like a practiced performance for a passive audience than a routine contribution woven into the ongoing pattern of alternating turns. So these personal anecdotes have consequences for the organization of surrounding turn-by-turn talk in ways rather different from canned jokes—a conclusion borne out in the analyses of stories Jefferson (1978) proposes.

Significantly, Jim accomplishes more than introducing the girl who received the letter Vera asked about with this initial anecdote. He begins to set the mood for the other story and gets his audience laughing. Moreover, as it turns out, Jim has no intention of moving right into the requested narrative about the letter, which turned out to be hardly a story at all; instead he takes advantage of the attention he now commands to tell a second intervening story. The passage above continues without pause or interruption as follows.

> JIM: In fact—she was the daughter of the woman who lived next door to my grandparents.
> VERA: Uhhunh.
> JIM: And er the couple, y'know. So we had such fun as kids and and it was she and her sister to whom I was exposing my brother's penis when my—
> TEDDY: [Hhuh.]
> VERA: [Haha] (h)I'm sure yeah.
> JIM: in the famous incident when my grandmother *broke* in on us and *shamed* me for life. Y'know really. I'll never forget this tre*men*dous weight of guilt. And "*Jim* what are you *do*ing."
> TEDDY: Huh huh huh.
> JIM: "*Come* out of there" y'know "*Girls* go home" and y'know.
> PAMELA: Wow.
> JIM: Then I remember just sitting in the livingroom with my grandparents y'know pointedly ignoring me.

VERA: Trying to act normally.

JIM: And just y'know making me feel terrible. And uh,

PAMELA: Oh.

TEDDY: Huh huh hehhehheh.

VERA: Ha ha ha ha ha ha ha.

JIM: But anyhow,

VERA: He took them in the bathroom and *showed* them his brother's.

PAMELA: Oh.

JIM: Uh heh heh.

VERA: "*Look* what he's got."

JIM: My brother didn't mind.

VERA: Yeah *huh* huh huh. His brother's younger than him.

PAMELA: Younger. Oh I see.

JIM: Yeah.

VERA: Hun huh.

JIM: Uh but—

VERA: Po(hoho)or kid. Huh huh huh.

PAMELA: Well.

VERA: "It's a *visual aid.* Here's my visual aid."

TEDDY: Huh *huh* huh *huh.* Yes. Show and tell. Yeah. "I'm bringing my brother's geni*tal*ia."

JIM: Huh huh huh huh huh.

VERA: Huh haha.

JIM: Hun huh huh [huh huh.]

PAMELA: [It sure is] nice to have a boy and a girl I tell you.

TEDDY: Yeah. Yeah.

JIM: Yeah.

VERA: Huh huh *huh huh huh.*

PAMELA: We won't have to show them anything.

JIM: [Right right.]

VERA: [That's right.]

JIM: Well I think y'know here were two sisters who didn't have a brother and two brothers who didn't have a sister and I think the idea was an exchange of [a kind—]

VERA: [You were] being an educator.

JIM: Yeah.

TEDDY: Sure.
JIM: But we were *rude*ly interrupted and
VERA: Eh huh huh huh huh huh.
JIM: So anyhow uh I just got to this cut-off point where suddenly I had to join the woman-haters' club.

Here at the end, Jim has finally begun to introduce the story about the letter per se, though further talk about children growing up will intervene before he gets to it this time. By virtue of Vera's request for a specific story, Jim thus has occasion to tell two thematically related anecdotes before even prefacing the letter story.

Again, in this second anecdote, Jim elicits laughter near the beginning with a brief statement of the story's point. He then proceeds to elaborate on this theme to the repeated amusement of his audience. His performance of the incident features dramatization of his grandmother's voice and his own state of contrition. As in the previous excerpt, the listeners join the fray once the initial laughter commences, each trying to concoct and insert some funny remark. Vera contributes to the dramatization with the line *Look what he's got* as if she were taking the part of one of the girls. Then she shifts gears and suggests a school scenario with *It's a visual aid.* Teddy picks up this cue in his mention of *show and tell.* The net effect approximates the banter we analyzed in the previous chapter, but there it clustered around conversational cruxes like openings, closings, and topic changes, while it attaches to an anecdote in the present case.

The structure we see here recurs in humorous personal anecdotes. The teller states the basic plot or theme of the narrative, then tells (and recycles) the story, dramatizing dialogue and stressing different aspects each time. Audience participation can ensue any time after the initial statement of the plot or theme. It usually begins with laughter, but once the listeners have laughed, they freely offer comments and invent dialogue of their own. Finally, the anecdote establishes a scene and characters which the audience and the teller then use as a backdrop for their respective humorous role-play and comment. Either the teller or a recipient may "formulate" the story in a "significance statement" which makes a moral point independent of the narrative proper; for more on the notion of formulation as it relates to narratives in Conversation Analysis, see Jefferson (1978) and Ryave (1978).

At the same time, the scene presents possibilities for serious discussion. Thus Pamela finds a reassuring moment in the anecdote, recalling that her two children, a boy and a girl, will not need to go next door for anatomy lessons. And this prompts Jim to formulate—in the sense just discussed—the main thrust of his narrative, recasting it in the somewhat more serious light of sex-education. Vera then draws out the personal relevance of the anecdote by noting that Jim—who is now in the teaching profession—was already *being an educator* in his early youth. We see here the power a recipient may excercise over the final interpretation of a story, as pointed out by Jefferson (1978), Ryave (1978), Sharrock and Turner (1978), Polanyi (1979), Goodwin (1986), and Spielman (1987). All this points up the function of personal anecdotes in presenting a particular personality, and ultimately in mutual revelation and ratification of self by the participants in talk.

We should also note the social control function of the story. The description and evaluation of the funny event reveal norms and attitudes the teller assumes his hearers share. He chooses the scientific term *penis* rather than a child's word like *wee-wee* or a potentially offensive name for the organ in question, which indicates a willingness to talk about such matters in appropriately neutral terminology, at the same time he implicitly criticizes his grandparents for their unsympathetic overreaction and guilt-based method of dealing with a child. So the anecdote has no butt like the joke proper, but it can certainly assign blame in various ways. And the revelation of such evaluations helps define appropriate behavior for participants in the group, including ways of speaking about potentially offensive matters.

A few minutes later, talk comes again to center on early sexual experience, as suggested by Jim's stories. In the excerpts below, two of the four participants tell a personal anecdote on this topic, and a third tries to, but cannot get the floor. Jim indirectly introduces the first anecdote by asking Vera about a matter she mentioned earlier. Then Vera prefaces the anecdote for Pamela with an initial statement of the story.

> JIM: Wh- what were you saying we ought to hear?
> VERA: Sara asked about *sex* today. Pretty directly.

PAMELA: In the car on the way to UPS.

VERA: Pamela's been wanting to tell this.

TEDDY: What'd she say?

PAMELA::   Completely- well, how does *sperm* get into my *tum*my. Into Mommy's tummy.

TEDDY: That's about sex, yeah. Heh heh heh.

JIM: Huh huh *huh* huh huh.

PAMELA: And I just went "Eeyou." {knocks over coffee cup}

VERA: Oh that's a *tough* one.

PAMELA: And y'know. It really was kinda *tough* to answer.

VERA: You were driving too, right?

PAMELA: Ha ha (h)yeah I was driving too.

VERA: Hhuh oh heh heh heh *heh* heh heh.

PAMELA: And we were in a hurry.

TEDDY: Yeah you knocked your coffee over just telling about [it. Huh huh huh.]

JIM: [Hahaha.]

VERA: Hahahahahahahaha. Heh heh heh heh *heh* heh heh heh.

TEDDY: Whoah.

PAMELA: It's more difficult to-

VERA: Do you need a napkin.

PAMELA: I do need *some*thing.

VERA: Let me get you something here.

PAMELA: Well I just told her you just have to *real*ly get close together. He he he he [heh heh heh heh.]

TEDDY: [Huh ha ha *ha* ha.]

JIM: Huh huh huh huh.

PAMELA: Why are you *laugh*ing. She was very- You have to *cud*dle and y'know. She didn't want to know more than that.

TEDDY: No they never do. That's the funny thing.

PAMELA: But ah thank you {to Vera for napkin} heh huh huh huh huh.

VERA: That sure would throw you. Huh huh huh *huh* huh huh.

TEDDY: My mom tells the story of having- She was *read*ing in the book-

PAMELA: This was so completely- I mean why? We were-

TEDDY: They never ask when you expect them to.

PAMELA: She didn't want to come with me to UPS.
TEDDY: No.
PAMELA: They were kind of having arguments upstairs and I
            said one of you will come with me, our guests will
            come in about twenty minutes, and here she (h)asks
            (h)me this que(he)stion and I was *"oh."* It was really
            cute.

Inasmuch as Vera has already produced her summary, Pamela has some trouble getting started, especially since Vera breaks back in to say that Pamela has been wanting to tell the story. Then Teddy turns the child's question into a joke with his understated *That's about sex, yeah,* before Pamela comes to her reaction and answer, which should make up the body of the story. Then, as noted above, the listeners feel free to begin inserting comments of their own, once they have laughed. Even worse, due to her animated performance, Pamela spills her coffee, which further breaks up the narrative, so that both Vera and Teddy interrupt repeatedly, both to keep the story moving and to get the coffee wiped up.

In fact, Teddy not only remarks about Pamela spilling her coffee, but also makes a bid to begin a story of his own, though Pamela wrests the floor back from him. Even then Teddy attempts to formulate the anecdote for Pamela, saying that children *never ask when you expect them to,* apparently as a way of leading into his own story on this related topic, a standard strategy described by Ryave (1978). But Pamela is not about to let someone else attach their own moral to her story and conclude it for her, so she recycles it one more time straight through. All the interruptions and the joint telling we observed constitute heavy but still acceptable audience participation in an anecdote, though they would absolutely ruin the performance of a normal narrative joke.

Despite all the unsolicited help Pamela receives in the telling, however, the anecdote remains hers. She finally regains control of the performance, and polishes it off with a nice summary and an evaluative comment: *It was really cute.* And this sort of evaluation is in line with the sympathetic attitude toward children's developing interest in human sexuality implied in the fore-going anecdote. For maximum effect in presenting a self, a personal narrative ought to describe not only a particular incident, but also the reaction and evaluation of the teller, as Labov and Waletzky (1967) argue. Especially in an anecdote where a parent describes something a child did, rather than something from her own childhood as in the examples so far, the response counts most. In spite of the way Pamela represents her momentary surprise and embarrassment at her daughter's question, she can draw back and perceive the whole event as *cute* in closing, which of course tells the audience far more about Pamela than about how little kids become acquainted with the birds and bees.

The final humorous anecdote I would like to consider comes from the same recorded interaction, and it reflects the ongoing topic of how children acquire information about human sexuality. Teddy finishes up some serious discussion, estimating the age at which he became interested in girls, when Jim breaks into his story.

TEDDY:	Early teens. Twelve, thirteen probably. Fourteen.
JIM:	When I was in the seventh grade somebody sold me a- one of these soft *art* erasers under the pre- telling me it was a *con*dom y'know hahahaha. And I was [*cur*ious]
TEDDY:	[Huh huh huh.]
JIM:	y'know to see what it was like. And uh "I don't see how you *use* this."
VERA:	What (h)was (h)it? (h)It was an er*a*(ha)ser?
JIM:	Yeah. A real *soft* eraser. Y'know the kind that you can- (0.7) that's malleable.
VERA:	Huh huh huh *huh* huh huh huh.
TEDDY:	Huh (h)But (h)not (h)that (h)malle(h)able.
JIM:	Right. Right.
TEDDY:	Huhhuhhuhhuh.
VERA:	Ah ha ha ha ha.
PAMELA:	Huh huh huh huh huh. That's cute.
VERA:	Your parents never *did* tell you anything though, did they?

Jim himself laughs as he finishes his initial statement of the anecdote, and elicits counter-laughter from Teddy before going on to describe his reaction and to dramatize his embarrassment. Vera laughs in disbelief rather than mirthfully as she requests more information about the offending eraser. Once Jim identifies for Vera the sort of eraser he means, she laughs for real, while Teddy moves into the comment section of the anecdote performance with his laughing *But not that malleable.* Pamela caps this performance with laughter and the same evaluation *cute* that characterized her own anecdote. And Jim seems satisfied enough with this assessment to let it stand unmodified.

It is especially significant for our treatment of personal anecdote telling as *mutual* revelation that Pamela's final remark stands as the only explicit evaluative comment on the story from the adult perspective. Of course, Jim's laughter at the end of his initial statement implicitly expresses his current attitude toward the incident, but he might easily have taken exception to Pamela's wrap-up, if only to reclaim his anecdote with a final formulation or evaluation of his own, as Pamela herself did in the foregoing example. Clearly, then, we can present a self by evaluating anecdotes others tell as well as our own. And we can acquiesce in the judgment of others, just as we can disagree with them, all of which provides relevant social data about the teller and the audience.

Telling humorous personal anecdotes helps present a self in several ways at once. First, tellers relate a chunk of their experience for the audience to consider in sizing them up. Second, they adopt a humorous stance toward this experience, which shows that they have a sense of humor about themselves, that they can now laugh about something initially difficult or painful for them. Third, beyond the humorous stance, the teller can comment evaluatively on the experience described. At the same time, recipients present lines of their own through their participation—by laughing with sympathy or *Schadenfreude,* by commenting philosophically or sarcastically, and, as the floor becomes available, by becoming subsequent tellers, while the former teller turns listener. Anecdote swapping thus nurtures rapport through sharing experience and sharing laughter at ourselves. Talking about our separate experiences makes them our common (at least vicarious) experiences, and laughing together makes our interaction enjoyable and memorable. So the personal anecdote rates high on the scales of self-presentation and rapport, and low on the scale of testing, though it succeeds in eliciting relevant social data from audience participation in the form of laughter, evaluative comment, and, finally, counter-anecdotes.

Jointly Produced Narratives

We have seen how the structure of the personal anecdote invites laughter and comment after an initial statement of its point. And we investigated several examples in which listeners so involved themselves in the progress of the narrative that they practically become co-tellers. In the final excerpt, the original teller even concurs with the concluding evaluation a recipient attaches to his anecdote. Precisely because a personal anecdote relates personal experience, however, it belongs to some individual—or in some cases to a couple or group who shared the experience in question, in which case a situation of genuine co-telling may arise. But we also find cases where two or more conversationalists participate more or less equally in constructing a narrative about some event they experienced separately. And, of course, they may produce a humorous narrative, either because the event is funny in its own right or because they adopt a funny perspective on it.

   To concretize the discussion, I would like to look at a passage in which Frank and Ned are reconstructing the story of the film *Mr. Roberts*. The exchange originates in a set of tapes I have drawn from in the preceding chapter: Ned and his family are spending a long weekend at the home of his parents, Frank and Lydia, along with the family of his brother Brandon. But at this particular time Frank and Ned are alone in the den, Ned leafing through a movie book and asking Frank about various titles as he comes to them. Frank ends up supplying most of the narrative thread in the following, since he has seen the film more recently, but Ned dramatizes the central incident and takes only one less speaking turn overall.

NED: But he's the all rules an-

FRANK: Ah he was a son of a bitch and he had a potted palm tree that sat up on the *bridge*. And it was (h)the huhhuh Jack Lemmon's job to come by and water that thing y'know an-

NED: But what does Lemmon finally do, does he throw it overboard?

FRANK: Yeah. He just got so goddamn-

NED: He was- says "I'm gonna-"

FRANK: got so goddamn mad he just-

NED: "To *hell* with this plant."

FRANK: Huh *huh* huh huh. He just took it huhh. Threw it over huh huh. And the *men* all watched him do it of course and everybody just,

NED: Huh huh huhhuh.

FRANK: Hyah hyah hyah. And then the old man then lined them all up and he was gonna huh huh huh draw and quarter all of them until he got a confe(he)ss(h)ion of who di(hi)d (h)it huh huh (h)y'know huhhuhhuh-huh and Lemmon stepped forward and, "*I* threw your *god damn plant* [overboard."]

NED: [Huh huh huh] huh.

FRANK: Hu hu hu hu huh huh huh huh.

NED: So you can look up in here anyway not just *guys* (4.0) y'know look up movies.

As in the anecdotes we looked at, the scenes depicted are funny in their own right, so the narrative does not build to a punch line, as it would in a canned joke, and laughter can occur anytime after the initial statement of the plot by Frank right in his first sentence. Since, furthermore, the story is not a personal narrative belonging to either participant, Frank feels free to laugh even as he continues his telling, and both men feel free to add details and dialogue.

Not only does this exchange lack a joke-style punch line, it also lacks the sort of formulation or evaluative comment we found at the conclusion of our personal anecdotes. Neither do we see the co-tellers pay any further attention to the characters they described nor the issues they raised in their jointly produced narrative, once they revert to regular turn-by-turn talk. This again contrasts with the personal anecdotes, after which talk often addresses the story or its teller. Once they have recalled and laughed over the central comic scenes of the film, Frank and Ned return to serious conversation about the movie book that prompted their concern with *Mr. Roberts* in the first place.

The only relevant personal data exchanged in this joint performance consists in the sort of personal information we signal almost any time we talk, namely films we have enjoyed, scenes we recall, and so on. And co-telling a narrative cannot function as much of a test of either understanding or memory, since each participant may fill in what the other has forgotten: Ned even asks for confirmation of his recollection that Lemmon threw the palm tree overboard. Joint production aligns the participants together, rather than setting up a teller on one side and an audience on the other. Consequently, the passage illustrates excellent conversational rapport. Frank and Ned conspire to relate scenes from a movie they have both seen, though not together. They agree on what scenes to relate and effectively negotiate the telling of them. Their rapid-fire turn exchanges and overlaps attest to their high level of involvement. Each laughs about the way the other dramatizes events and finally about their joint performance overall. So they succeed in making their separate past experiences into a common experience, which represents a fundamental mechanism of rapport through talk.

Wordplay

If we achieve rapport by turning our separate personal experiences into shared experience, and if jointly produced narratives and personal anecdotes allow us to accomplish this along with amusing each other and laughing together, then certainly these two sorts of talk exchanges must range quite high among our strategies for creating conversational rapport. Wordplay, by contrast, though it aims to elicit amusement and laughter, carries little or no weight as personal experience. Again, personal anecdotes present a self with a particular past and particular ways of evaluating it, so that they often lead into serious talk about the teller, various assessments of the event at issue, and the event itself. On the other hand, we do not invest much by way of our past or our evaluations of it in wordplay, which consequently displays a witty but otherwise hardly individualized self and, hence, provides no grist to the mill of serious topical talk. The effect of engaging in regular wordplay is to present a general self-image of someone willing to suspend the conversational business at hand for a laugh, of someone attentive to the form of talk and its potential for playful manipulation as well as for communication proper. Furthermore, wordplay may take on the character of a competitive game for some conversationalists, especially those who maintain a customary joking relationship with certain other individuals or groups. Such speakers may keep a kind of unofficial tally of successful joking and repartee with each other, so that for any given conversation or stretch of time each knows who has scored more points in the humor competition, whether they are gaining or losing ground with respect to each other, and so on.

Punning in particular enjoys a rather poor reputation traditionally: Puns count as frivolous and superficial even as vehicles of humor, and certainly contribute nothing to the ongoing conversation. Like the telling of a narrative joke, a pun constitutes a little showcase with a single conversationalist performing for the others. Further, as Sherzer (1978) points out, puns disrupt topical talk by misconstruing and redirecting it. By contrast with personal anecdotes and jointly produced narratives, puns rank quite high on the scale of aggression and testing. We do not announce puns or preface them as we do anecdotes and canned jokes. We cannot ask if our listener has heard the one about so and so, because puns grow out of the immediate context of talk. They test our attention to this context, and our ability to reanalyze the talk within it rapidly, as well as our ability to take a joke in some cases.

Of course, we test for more than attention to context and analytic aptitude with our wordplay. We may play on rather marginal senses of a word, those related to arcane or abstract areas of knowledge. And we may play on more or less covert sexual and religious connotations of words and phrases. So we gather insight into the background knowledge of our listeners, and also into their attitudes toward and tolerance about potentially embarrassing and taboo areas. Wordplay has no monopoly on this sort of insight, of course: Personal anecdotes and canned jokes can and often do touch on sensitive topics like politics, religion, and sexuality. But the allusions in wordplay are better camouflaged, more easily denied, and hence more effective tools of reconnaissance.

Moreover, wordplay may become the primary activity during some stretches of conversation, or it may amount to an undercurrent which foams up to the surface occasionally. For some conversationalists, and especially for some pairs or larger groups in frequent contact, wordplay provides a recurrent cohesive element of their interactions. It may also serve to get talk started, to fill uncomfortable pauses, and to negotiate topic changes and closing, as we saw in the preceding chapter. So wordplay can be a game some conversationalists engage in within their larger interaction to render it smoother and more entertaining; it can keep them on their respective conversational toes just as it keeps them on the same shared wavelength, and thereby enhance rapport between them. In the following, I would like to explore these suggestions about the interpersonal functions of wordplay.

Punning

Recall from the preceding chapter the interactional description of puns as skewed responses to foregoing talk. The punster constructs an ambivalent utterance with one meaning oriented toward understanding the preceding utterance and a second meaning also fitted to that utterance but based on a contextually inappropriate analysis of it—which is roughly the definition of the pun Sacks (1973:139) offers. The punning turn consequently clashes with the topic and/or tenor of current conversation, while some linguistic element establishes its claim to a rather tenuous formal relevance. Thus, in the passage below, again involving three undergraduate student assistants in the departmental copying room, talk shifts abruptly from the concrete activity of cutting paper to Arnold's mental condition via the fortuitous connection between the concrete and mental senses of the phrase *off center.*

ARNOLD: An exact cut. (2.5) Oh no. This one is a little off
          center.
JUDY: That's because you're a little off center.
BETH: Heh *heh* he heh.
ARNOLD: No it's Tom's print.

Judy expropriates a phrase Arnold initially introduced with literal reference to some papers he is cutting, then applies it to Arnold himself, so that it takes on its figurative sense. She lets the dual meaning potential of Arnold's phrase *off center* entice her into a punning attack on him. This points up one sort of verbal aggression often associated with puns: The punster moves into an antagonistic relationship with one or more listeners, thus realigning the participants in the conversation. This attack differs from the rather mild aggression associated with puns as little understanding tests, according to Sherzer (1978), not only in severity but also in the clear aim it takes at an individual. Judy may be testing Beth, in the sense of Sherzer, to see if she gets the joke, but she puts Arnold to a more severe test to see if he can retain his composure and to reply in kind. Judy may routinely launch verbal assaults on her interlocutors or she may limit her attacks to Arnold and a few others with whom she enjoys what we are calling a customary joking relationship. Either way, verbal aggression of this sort reveals something of the personality Judy chooses to express and her relationship with Arnold; at the same time, Arnold's failure to respond at all provides relevant, though initially ambiguous, social data about him, as discussed above.

Puns occur most obviously in the second position of an adjacency pair, where expectations about appropriate responses serve to highlight the punning twist. In the last chapter we saw a stock, traditional example of just such a punning response in the pair: *Are you coming? – No just breathing hard.* The first pair part consists of a question conventionally used to ask about someone's plans or state of readiness, while the response takes the question to refer to sexual activity. So the answer ends up with only spurious phonological relevance to the original question. In interpersonal terms, the punning response represents a refusal to respond appropriately to a straightforward request for information, and an attempt to change the topic through the introduction of potentially objectionable subject matter, over and above whatever aggression the pun itself involves. All this should threaten the face of the first speaker and violate the principles of politeness as described by Lakoff (1973, 1982) and Brown and Levinson (1978), according to which failure to respond to civil requests for so-called free goods and services is an imposition on the person making the request. Nevertheless, by using humor, the person responding goes "off record," so that the first speaker need register neither the imposition nor the face threat. Furthermore, if humor allows us to talk off record, it provides us with a way of accomplishing certain conversational aims without strict accountability. And this helps explain the presence of something as disruptive and potentially uncomfortable as punning in conversation.

Punning thus does have some redeeming social value to counterbalance all its disruption of talk, its near imposition and impoliteness. It provides a way of talking off record, so that we can manipulate the flow of topics, test for relevant social data, and realign participants in nonconfrontational ways. Nor should we overlook the entertainment we derive from punning with its consequent enhancement of rapport from demonstrating shared background knowledge and laughing together, with the competitive game environment it creates, and, hence, the opportunity it affords us for the presentation of a witty self. We should keep an eye out for these functions of punning and wordplay in the examples to come.

The next excerpt exemplifies the effects of a pun in the response slot of an adjacency pair in spontaneous conversation. It shows how the skewed relevance of punning suggests a new direction for talk at odds with what has gone before. Once again the passage involves Frank and Lydia, their son Ned and his wife, Claire, and another son, Ned's brother, Brandon. Frank has offered to fill up Ned's gas tank for him, and on his way out to the garage Frank wants to determine whether he should check the oil as well. Under normal circumstances, and especially in this context, the question *How's your oil* clearly relates to its level rather than its quality, which sets the stage for Ned's reply in terms of the latter.

FRANK: How's your oil? Have you checked your oil.

NED: My oil is great.

LYDIA: *Huh* huh huh huh.

FRANK: How is your coolant.

NED: Ha My(hy) coolant is great too.

CLAIRE: You *ne*ver *check* it.

NED: I check them *so* often

CLAIRE: Because I'm on his back. "Don't you *think* we (h)hafta che(he)ck the oil and the coolant. *Nah*neh *nah*neh."

NED: I check the oil about every say fifteen or twe(hehe)nty (h)*min*utes.

CLAIRE: [I wish you'd show me how to] do it.

BRAD: [Huh huh huh huh huh huh huh.]

NED: Huh heh heh heh. Huh huh huh huh. Huh (h)I just che(he)ck—

BRANDON: Every day.

NED: Huh ha ha ha ha ha ha ha.

FRANK: Now let me tell you. As recently as four weeks ago. Or less than that. *Two* weeks ago I became aware that it seemed that my engine was running just a tad warmer than usual. . . .

Ned's punning response leads to laughter, and establishes a play frame, in the sense of Bateson (1953) and Fry (1963). Far from taking offense at Ned's blatant refusal to answer the question he intended, Frank seems willing to act the part of the stooge, and feeds Ned another straight line to extend the pun. Then Claire enters the fray with hyperbole, which sets off histrionics between her and Ned built around their differing attitudes on the care and maintenance of the family car. Their parody presentation of a squabbling couple works as a presentation of self on several levels simultaneously. Once Ned and Brandon run the hyperbolic role-play into the ground, Frank introduces a story suggested by the discussion of fluid levels in automobiles, rather than leaving for the gas station as he claimed he was about to do. So this excerpt points up the power puns have to redirect the flow of talk *and* action. Not only does the pun suggest a new topic, it also introduces a play frame which orients participants toward further joking. The cumulative effect of these two factors often alters the alignment of participants as well as changing the topic.

At the same time, the passage shows the sort of role-play often associated with puns: The punster pretends to have misunderstood something in the foregoing utterance, here the gist of Frank's question about oil. This differs significantly from the role-play Claire and Ned engage in just afterwards, where they conspire to produce a caricature of themselves. Further, the pun reacts directly to and reflects back on foregoing talk, whereas the role-play of hyperbole or irony may be self-contained. A single conversationalist may thus employ hyperbole or irony within the scope of a single turn and without consequences for preceding talk, while punning, as defined here, always represents a reaction to a previous turn and requires the listener to go back and reanalyze it to discover a new interpretation. Nevertheless, as the foregoing example illustrates, both punning and hyperbole can provide the basis for an interactional sequence. In fact, conversationalists routinely engage in bouts of hyperbole, allusion, and extended metaphor as well as punning. Some of the group dynamics of all these types of humor come out in the following passages.

Let us first investigate a passage where an initial pun provides the basis for several turns of wordplay. Here again Jason and his wife, Margaret, are at the home of Trudy and Roger for dinner. The four are seated at the table over dessert and coffee, and Jason is describing a painting.

JASON:	That painting in our livingroom of the *boat* in the—
MARGARET:	Yawl in the channel? Maine?
JASON:	There's a little boat and an island.
ROGER:	Y'all in the channel? Huhhuh.
JASON:	Yawl. [Yawl.]
MARGARET:	[It's a] boat, y'all.
ROGER:	What are y'all doing in the channel. Huh huh huh.
MARGARET:	I need a little port.
ROGER:	Huh huh huh *huh* huh.
TRUDY:	Haw haw haw haw.

MARGARET: Y'all in that channel huh huh huh. What are y'all
           in that channel for. I know.
   ROGER: Sorry. Who painted yawl in the channel?
   JASON: It's a painting by a painter named . . .

This pun picks out a word in the preceding turn for humorous
comment, rather than filling the second slot of an adjacency pair,
so it lacks one prong of the aggression seen in the previous
example. Nevertheless, it violates our expectations for sequential
relevance by forcibly yoking the noun *yawl* with the Southern
personal pronoun *y'all* based on their fortuitous phonological
identity. Roger marks his pun with a final laugh, but Jason treats
it as a legitimate failure to understand, repeating the crucial word
by way of clarification. Margaret picks up on the pun, and produces a parallel utterance. Note, however, that Margaret's *It's a*
boat, y'all cannot count as a pun itself, since it maintains the
sense of the previous turn, though it surely illustrates wordplay
and even role-play in its attempt to imitate Southern speech
patterns. By the same reasoning, we must consider Roger's repetition of *y'all* in the next turn wordplay and role-play, but not
a pun as such. Then Margaret delivers *I need a little port* in such
a manner that it sounds more like a request for a drink than an
explanation of someone's presence in a channel, and that *does*
amount to a pun, before she recycles *y'all in the channel.*
Margaret and Roger spar verbally as a basic part of their interactional routine, and Margaret seems here to take advantage of
the first opportunity she spies to redress the perceived imbalance
with a pun of her own. One pun leads to another, not only
because it establishes a play frame and prompts participants to
work out secondary meanings for apparently appropriate utterances, but also because punning is a competitive game for those
conversationalists who engage in it regularly.

It is worthy of note that Roger, who instigated the wordplay,
also returns to topical talk with a question directed to the interrupted speaker. In saying *sorry* Roger apologizes either for the
poor quality of the initial pun, for the interruption, or perhaps
for both. Jason's silence may have prompted this reaction; after
all, he neither laughed nor took a speaking turn after his
attempted clarification. Just because humor is technically off rec-

ord, this does not prevent it from being an unwelcome inter-ruption to the speaker who lost the floor or a shock to the sensibilities of participants who feel the humor and laughter intrude frivolously into sacrosanct matters. And precisely such reactions provide examples of the "relevant social data" dis-cussed above. In any case, the turn segues back into Jason's description of a painting. So we see that participants in talk may themselves recognize the aggressive and disruptive effect of pun-ning, and attempt to ameliorate it and return to the flow of topical conversation which occasioned the initial pun.

To summarize briefly, in punning we analyze a stretch of fore-going speech in two ways, and respond to the interpretation which is *in*congruent with the current context. This doubly dis-rupts topical talk, first in suggesting a new topic with spurious claim to relevance, and second in introducing a play frame, which makes more punning and other sorts of wordplay appropriate. Other participants may construct puns of their own, they may manipulate the phrasing of the original pun, and they may move into alternate sorts of wordplay, any or all of which at least postpones and potentially obliterates further topical talk. Puns serve to display wit and test for shared knowledge and attitudes; and they awake a competitive urge in those individuals who make wordplay a part of their personal conversational style. Besides the relatively mild aggression associated with puns as understanding tests, we observed a more threatening potential for aggression directed at a particular person or group in punning. In addition, interlocutors may take offense at the interruption and/or frivolity of punning in some cases. Still, as a form of wordplay, punning generally contributes to the enjoyment of the talk exchange and enhances rapport, especially for speakers who actively participate in a competitive customary joking re-lationship.

Wordplay Interaction

We have seen how punning can lead to various sorts of verbal gymnastics and role-play. Once a pun has introduced a play frame, all kinds of humor become acceptable. And this holds for wordplay generally. In the passage below, again from the recordings made during a long weekend the two brothers, Ned and Brandon, and their families spent at the home of their parents, Frank and Lydia, Frank establishes a humorous key with hyperbole, first in his choice of aeronautical vocabulary like *takeoff* and *payload,* then in his grossly exaggerated *twenty tons,* though no laughter ensues till he commences his claim to have *never seen an insect that big.* And the play frame takes firm hold when Ned and Brandon begin suggesting names for the insect from inappropriate categories. Frank enlists Brandon as a witness to his hyperbole, then extends his aeronautical metaphor, using the specifically aircraft term *fuselage* twice and *wingspan* once. Finally, he puts an end to his own extended metaphor and hyperbole in offering an objectively appropriate comparison with a hummingbird.

NED: I keep hearing people call them things like hornets.

FRANK: Let me tell you. That dude was big enough to take off with a payload of about twenty tons.

NED: Well what do you call it?

FRANK: I didn't know what to call it. I had never seen [an insect] that big. Ever.

NED: [He he.]

FRANK: The only thing I could think to [call it—]

NED: [He he] he he Call it, "get thee hence." Hehheh.

BRANDON: Call it sir.

NED: Heh heh *heh* heh hehhehheh.

FRANK: Let me tell you what I call it. "My God look at that big bug." It had a fuselage *that* big. {holds up fingers}

NED: Ehhehheh *ha* ha ha.

FRANK: Yeah. Brandon, I'm not exaggerating, am I?

BRANDON: Oh no. No. Easy.

FRANK: It had a fuselage like *that.*

NED: Eh huh huh huh.

FRANK: And a wingspan like *that.* Oh man. Never seen [one like that.]

NED: [So we're talking] primordial here.

FRANK: It was just slightly smaller than a hummingbird.

Of particular interest here for the analysis of the interpersonal dimension is the way participants take turns in making contributions to the humorous framework once established. All three men take a shot at naming the bug and commenting hyperbolically on its size. The conspiracy reaches its high point when Frank appeals to Brandon for testimony that he is not exaggerating, and Brandon goes even one step further in saying *Oh no. No. Easy.* At the end, even Ned kicks in *primordial* as a show of solidarity. The net effect parallels that of the jointly produced description of humorous scenes from the movie *Mr. Roberts,* which we analyzed above. Here the three participants succeed, as a group, in describing a past event only two of them experienced firsthand, but this time they have to make the event funny themselves via extended metaphor, hyperbole, and allusion. Consequently, we see here also a degree of role-play to make the hyperbole work which was unnecessary in relating the movie scenes which the men found funny in their own right. So the payoff in terms of entertainment and rapport should be even greater.

Notice also that Brandon's *call it sir* echoes a line from an old riddle joke, one version of which goes as follows:

QUESTION: What do you call a seven-foot, three-hundred-pound bully armed to the teeth?
ANSWER: Sir.

The allusion works on several levels at once in conversational humor. First of all, conversationalists gain prestige any time they can successfully weave an allusion into the fabric of spontaneous conversation. According to Freud (1905), we derive a childlike pleasure from the serendipity of finding old acquaintances in new environments. So even unfunny allusion can excite a laugh of recognition and a moment of rapport between participants in a conversation, because they can bask in their shared ability to identify the relevant piece of preexisting text.

Further, reference to a joke makes Brandon's line a special type of allusion for purposes of conversational humor. Allusion to a text funny in itself has an obvious double humorous potential, first in its actual contribution to the current text, and second by recalling the original text for listeners in the know. Moreover, in the present case, the original joke revolves around a pun. In the question, *what do you call* has the force of 'how do you designate', whereas *sir* in the answer reanalyzes the question as something like 'how do you address'. So Brandon's turn also works as a pun itself along with the allusion and wordplay proper based on the inappropriateness of *sir* as a class name. Finally, the allusion is especially apt in its reference to a rather large member of the species as well, so that it works on several levels simultaneously.

Any unannounced intertextual reference or allusion poses an understanding test, which can elicit laughter and enhance rapport in its own right. And Brandon's turn combines allusion with punning and wordplay, so it should pose a compound test. Interestingly, Ned responds to the test immediately and appreciatively, while Frank fails to react to it, perhaps because he was intent on delivering his own line, though he may simply have been unfamiliar with the joke in question as well. This appreciation for a witty allusion and the differential reaction to it are the sorts of data participants take more or less conscious note of, and they ultimately accrue to the personalities conveyed in humorous conversational interaction. We shall see more allusion in the next example, and go into more detail on it there.

The following passage again thrives on intertextual references, and it returns us to the dinner table for dessert with the host couple, Trudy and Roger, and their guests, Margaret and Jason, familiar from previous examples. Roger instigates the allusion and role-play with a broad parody of a cinematic stereotype Mexican, apparently not from any particular film. Though this performance elicits no laughter, it does cue Jason's reference to a passage recognizably from *Crocodile Dundee*. Jason needs only deliver the first half of the speech with appropriate gestures and a mock-Australian accent for Roger to be able to follow closely and complete the couplet with him. Then Margaret follows up with her own version of the whole speech.

MARGARET: Where's a knife for the cheesecake.
ROGER: Here this'll do. {offering corkscrew}
JASON: Hoo *heh* heh heh heh heh.

MARGARET: Oh God.
ROGER: Here. {folding out small blade}
JASON: Heh heh heh heh *ha* ha ha ha.
ROGER: "Hey, you wanna knife Gringo? Here's a knife."
JASON: "That's not a knife,"
ROGER: What kind of a—huh huh huh (h)yeah.
JASON: "*This* is a [*knife.*" Heh heh heh.]
ROGER: ["*This* is a *knife*" huh huh *huh*]
JASON: Huh huh huh huh [huh *huh* huh huh huh huh huh.]
ROGER: [What kind of a knife] do you want?
MARGARET: "That's not a knife? Now *that's* a knife." {brandishing real knife}
JASON: Heh heh heh.

Jason, of course, gets the credit for the allusion per se, though Roger "shadows" his words closely, in the sense of Tannen (1987), and finishes it up almost simultaneously with him. But there is method in Jason's pausing at the caesura in the allusion. He not only provides Roger with an opportunity to signal recognition of the crucial line based on minimal surrounding text, but also lets him participate in the performance. This sort of joint production makes for very high rapport interaction, as we have seen in preceding examples and discussion. If Roger had not reacted so rapidly, Jason would probably have simply completed the allusion himself with no loss of face for Roger. Thus Jason sets up a situation where everyone wins, both in demonstrating common background knowledge and in sharing the honors of performing. For more on the matter of how humorous texts relate to prior texts, how parody works, and related issues, see Norrick (1989).

We have been investigating the interactional dynamics of extended metaphor, hyperbole, and allusion. Once one participant in a conversation begins any kind of wordplay, it introduces a play frame which sets the stage for further play by others. This often results in an interaction where participants take turns contributing funny lines to the ongoing discourse, and it may involve joint production as such. Either way, participants have a chance to perform for the group, to test for and demonstrate shared background knowledge and attitudes, and to enjoy laughing together. The effect is one of heightened rapport.

Of course, allusion, hyperbole, metaphor, and irony often also inform a single turn with no effect on the interaction besides the laughter they elicit in the immediately following turn space. For the sake of completeness, since we have not inspected an example of irony yet, let us consider the following passage, which takes us back to a discussion between the brothers Brandon and Ned at the home of their parents. The two are discussing movies, when Ned invokes irony in the narrow sense of *mentioning* a proposition opposite what he believes and hopes to convey, as in the analysis by Sperber and Wilson (1981).

> BRANDON: I watched The Fountainhead just a couple weeks ago. With Gary Cooper and Patricia Neal—
> NED: Boy I'll bet *that's* a great movie.
> BRANDON: I(hi)t's a t(h)errible movie hehhehheh.
> NED: Huh huh. [Huh huh huh.]
> BRANDON: [It was pretty] *good.* I had read the book. . . .

Ned's straightforwardly ironic *I'll bet that's a great movie* elicits more laughter than it seems to deserve, but it has little effect on the conversation otherwise. Brandon reverts immediately to the literal *terrible,* rather than joining in the ironic approach, and proceeds to his description of the film. Here again, then, the effects of the wordplay end with the expected laughter in the following turn. Irony seems to generate further humorous talk less frequently than does hyperbole or punning, perhaps because it has come to be an unmarked form of expression for many speakers. In addition, this construction or mentioning of statements opposite to the opinion one holds seems too obvious by itself to count as much of an understanding test for recipients of irony. For these reasons, irony does little to present a self or to gain credit for conversationalists who use it. A possible exception may occur among partners in a customary joking relationship, which dictates that they capitalize on any opportunity for humorous aggression. In fact, much of the effect of irony often rests on the caustic comment it conveys, as seems to be the case in the passage just above.

In this regard, recall the initial example cited in the preceding section, where Judy takes a comment about an *off-center* paper cut as her cue to verbally attack the speaker, saying *That's because you're a little off center.* There, too, the sarcastic comment it levels against someone present accounts for the laughter it excites as much as the force of the pun itself. Direct on-record affronts like this so obviously flout the norms of politeness, according to Lakoff (1973) and Brown and Levinson (1978), that they strike us as funny, just as the incongruity of a president's pratfall or a talking dog might. Paradoxically, flying in the face of friendly politeness can build rapport, because it signals a relationship which eschews such superficial conventions, as we shall see below. This sort of sarcastic wordplay to mock the foregoing speaker and its interpersonal significance make up a central concern of the next section.

Sarcasm and Mocking

The Virginian, hero of Wister's novel of the same name, lets his friend Steve jokingly call him a son-of-a-bitch twice, to the amazement of the narrator. But the same phrase from an unsmiling stranger at a poker game immediately brings out the Virginian's six-shooter and the famous phrase, "When you call me that, smile," which causes the stranger to back down. A smile or some other signal may initiate a joking frame, and it may be in force by default in interactions between friends, especially those who view themselves as partners in a customary joking relationship; but we are well advised to avoid randomly calling people sons of bitches or attacking them verbally in any way—especially when they have a loaded gun under the card table. In fact, sarcasm and mocking initially seem directly contrary to normal conventions of politeness and rational cooperation in conversation. A brief consideration of recent thinking on these matters seems appropriate here.

Grice (1975) proposed that we adhere to a Cooperative Principle and a set of so-called "conversational maxims" derived from it in our talk exchanges. He argued that listeners draw inferences about intended meanings based on the maxims and on the assumption that speakers are observing the Cooperative Principle generally even when they violate a maxim. Grice further suggested other social maxims which help regulate our interactions as well, for example politeness conventions.

Lakoff (1973) determined that the Cooperative Principle itself followed from the basic tenets of politeness: In particular, if we are to avoid imposing on others, we must see to it that we say what we have to say as briefly, coherently, and accurately as possible. Moreover, Lakoff suggested that listeners infer speaker intentions based on the principles of politeness, again on the assumption that the speakers are interacting accountably even when they violate those principles.

Brown and Levinson (1978) investigated the interaction of politeness conventions with the notion of "face" à la Goffman (1955) in a range of cultures. They found universally in various admixtures both "positive" politeness, related to "positive face" and thus involving ratification of the other people's good feelings about themselves, and "negative" politeness, related to "negative face" and thus to other people's desire to be left alone. Positive politeness strategies include signs of "solidarity": acting friendly, making compliments, and the like; negative politeness consists in recognition of "power": acting respectful, maintaining distance, giving options, and the like.

Tannen (1986) demonstrates what she calls the "paradox of power and solidarity," whereby a single turn at talk allows dual interpretations in line with both power/negative politeness and with solidarity/positive politeness. Thus a friendly greeting shows solidarity, but at the same time it implies a lack of distance and respect; a compliment on a new car from someone who already has one can show solidarity, but it can also appear deprecating. Consequently, according to this paradox, acting *dis*respectful can signal solidarity, just as it can signal real aggression, while acting too polite and complimentary can begin to make the recipient feel uneasy—which, finally, brings us to the interpersonal significance of sarcasm.

By Tannen's paradox of power/solidarity, a verbal attack can signal solidarity, because it implies a relationship where distance, respect, and power count for little. If we can do without the overt trappings of positive politeness, and freely poke fun at each other, we must enjoy good rapport. This attitude naturally leads to the sort of customary joking relationship mentioned above, and it may merge into what Tannen (1990) calls ritual combat. Close friends and family members can afford to eschew the more obvious demonstrations of mutual respect and affection associated with public behavior, because they share a private bond. They may choose to express their intimacy in argument and witty repartee, rather than in the polite forms they prefer with outsiders. So a *meta*message of "this is play," in the sense of Bateson (1953), accompanies the impolite, antagonistic message expressed in the audible conversation itself. This strategy informs the "conversational style"—to use Tannen's term—of some individuals, groups, and entire cultures. Schiffrin (1984) shows how arguing can work as a primary device for sociality among Jews in close contact with one another. Combined with skill in wordplay, which displays wit and yields amusement, this strategy shapes the interactions of those who follow it, and it looms large in the specific personalities they present.

The last example illustrated irony in the narrow sense, where *I'll bet that's a great movie* conveyed that Ned thought the film was bad. According to the analysis by Sperber and Wilson (1981), however, irony includes remarks like *If you want to get in the dishwasher* in the next excerpt, where Joe cannot reasonably expect Lynn to take advantage of his proposal. As a guest at the home of her friend, Joe, and his younger sisters, Penny and Gail, Lynn sets the stage for Joe's barb by offering to dry dishes before she realizes the others are loading them into the dishwasher. From their point of view, then, Lynn's offer is inappropriate, and Joe's suggestion reframes it as irrational.

LYNN:	Do you need me to help you dry?
JOE:	If you want to get in the *dish*washer.
PENNY:	Heh *heh* heh heh.
GAIL:	Huh huh oh yeah.
LYNN:	Oh you're putting them in the dishwasher. Okay.

GAIL: Oh gee.
PENNY: Gross.
JOE: Is that a seven layer salad there?

Lynn's offer would involve performing an activity which makes no sense in the present context; then Joe pokes fun at her willingness to help by suggesting a course of action in line with the lack of contextual information the offer entails. Joe's remark envisions a world in which Lynn can make good on her offer: This draws attention to her mistaken presumption and exacerbates it by describing its consequences. The image of sitting in a dishwashing machine to dry dishes is funny in itself, which renders Lynn's precipitous offer all the more laughable. Both here and in the foregoing example, the speakers "mention"—in the technical sense where "mentioning" contrasts with "using"—a proposition in tune with the words or spirit of their victims, but at odds with what they themselves believe. In the first case, the speaker asserted a proposition opposite what he believed, whereas in this second example Joe formulates a thought extrapolated from Lynn's offer to dry, namely that she might actually crawl inside the dishwasher.

Like the ironic statement *I bet that's a great movie* from the final passage in the previous section, the sarcastic remark here elicits laughter, but has no special effect on the immediately following talk. In fact, Lynn responds to it just as she might have to a serious reply like *No thanks we have a dishwasher.* And parallel to the punning sarcasm of *That's because you're a little off center* in an earlier example, Joe aims his remark directly at the previous speaker, though the scene he suggests certainly involves less aggression than the *off-center* cut. In both cases, however, according to the paradox of power/solidarity described above, the message of aggression carries with it a metamessage that the attack is only play and the participants are mutually engaged in a customary joking relationship; the example just below attests to the reflexivity of this relationship, as Lynn strikes back verbally at Joe. Of course, not every metamessage comes through loud and clear; and even when the metamessage is received intact, the recipient may still feel offended by clever sarcasm. The interpersonal dynamics of face-to-face talk are sufficiently complex to ensure that we always run a risk in mocking fellow participants for misjudging or misspeaking.

Reduced to its minimal form, mocking the preceding speaker for saying something wrong may consist in a simple repetition of the offending construction: see Norrick (1993a) for examples and analysis. Following speakers can repeat a slip of the tongue with question intonation, as Lynn does initially in the passage below, to request confirmation or correction by the first speaker. Or they can produce a verbatim repeat with level stress, as Penny does, to draw attention to the slip. And they may place the slip in a new context, as Lynn does the second time around, to exacerbate the error—a method Joe followed in the preceding example by describing consequences for Lynn's contextually inappropriate offer. Any of these strategies serves to highlight the error, embarrass the first speaker, and elicit laughter. Except for the initial question form, all the strategies also involve at least minimal wordplay, since the repeater acts as if the form were correct. However, since slips of the tongue are funny all by themselves, the mockers need not work very hard to elicit laughter. The passage below involves the same participants as the preceding one and follows it by a couple minutes.

> JOE: How much our shister *wastes* money,
> LYNN: Your *shis*ter?
> JOE: needlessly—
> PENNY: Our shister hehhehheh.
> GAIL: My *shis*ter Penny. Ha ha ha.
> PENNY: All right. Is that my wine glass. Heh heh *ha* ha ha.

Of course, the polite thing to do when someone produces a slip of the tongue or any other social faux pas is simply to ignore it and get on with the business at hand. Drawing attention to an error amounts to a potential affront, so even a verbatim repeat counts as mocking, just as pretending to limp in imitation of a lame person would. But again the metamessage comes across that this is just play, a competitive game Lynn and Joe agree to participate in as equals: They are engaged in a customary joking relationship requiring them to play the roles of ritual combatants—after all, Lynn has to pay Joe back for the sarcastic remark about her offer to dry dishes a few minutes earlier.

Before we leave the topic of mocking, we should not fail to recognize that it plays a role in group cohesion. Even such early writers on humor as Hutcheson (1750) and Bergson (1899) pointed out the force of laughter as a method of "social control." We poke fun at those who are different from us, but also at the foibles and slips of members within our own group; and in both cases our laughter aims at behaviors which we censure or at least seek to avoid. Thus joking and laughter help enforce group norms. And in spite of its initial aggression—indeed to a great extent because of it—mocking ends up identifying inappropriate forms of behavior for everyone present, including the person who was not paying attention or who made the error. Lynn failed to assess the dishwashing situation before blurting out her offer; *shister* does not meet the norm for acceptable pronunciation. These are far from serious infractions; they invite amusement, rather than outrage. But conversationalists did pick them out for special attention, and, even within a ritual combat setting, this shows concern with group norms and values, in particular the form of talk. This conjures up the metalingual function of joking, which makes up the central concern of the next chapter. So mocking has a regulative effect on a group. One source of relevant social data we can observe in a new person or a new group we come into contact with is the targets of their laughter. Another source of social data is, of course, how groups and participants respond to mocking. Certainly one way children determine norms is by hearing older kids and adults laugh about people and events that fail to conform in some way. Nothing helps us remember a social blunder like having been laughed at for it by a group of our peers—it definitely has more effect on children than would a serious reprimand. Thus mocking helps identify and enforce group norms.

By way of contrast with the foregoing examples where one conversationalist mocks another, let us look briefly at an example of what seems to be self-mocking. In the passage below, which again returns us to the evening Trudy and Roger had Margaret and Jason to dinner, Roger is offering Jason some aspirin for a headache. When he makes a comment about body weight and dosage, Jason seizes the opportunity for an apparently self-deprecating reference to his own bulk.

ROGER: Well do you want aspirin?
JASON: Yes. What are they.
ROGER: These are regular old. {shaking bottle} Regular, two? Or three.
JASON: Regular? I'll take three.
ROGER: At your body weight you need three.
JASON: Gimme *five.*
MARGARET: Huahahahaha.
TRUDY: Come on.
ROGER: I'm not talking about his *weight.* I'm just—I'm talking,
TRUDY: Um.
ROGER: At your *size.* Sorry.

Notice that *Gimme five* works in several ways at once: It overstates the request, and playfully recalls a hip request for a handshake, besides reflecting on Jason's weight, which elicits polite disagreement from Trudy with *Come on* and, with some urging by Trudy, a revised statement and perfunctory apology from Roger. So Jason can ratify cultural and group norms about being overweight through his own hyperbole, and perhaps thus shield himself against barbs from others. In fact, he may actually be fishing for compliments or at least for reassurance and understanding. Moreover, self-mocking works to present a sense of humor about oneself. As we saw in our investigation of embarrassing personal anecdotes, tellers ultimately gain credit for not taking themselves too seriously and for being able to overcome adversity. Self-mocking, then, ends up quite different from mocking and sarcasm directed at others. A humorous attack on oneself can hardly express real aggression, though it can serve to reiterate group opinion. What remains is the entertainment value for others and their empathy.

In the next chapter we shall see how humorous attention to matters of vocabulary and construction similarly tends to crystalize appropriate ways of speaking in the linguistic community and its subgroups. The last example gave us an inkling of how the mechanism works, though it revolved around a momentary slip in speech production, rather than the form of talk evolving in a group—like limping because your foot is asleep, rather than from some habitual behavior. Mocking and sarcasm, as we have seen, exploit either sort of error for their purposes. Especially in customary joking relationships, but also more generally, sarcasm and mocking can express both aggression and solidarity—aggression in the message, attacking others for their foibles and errors, and solidarity in the metamessage, including others in a playful relationship where we do not have to stand on formality. Self-mocking parallels telling embarrassing personal narratives: It allows us to ratify group values, and show we do not take ourselves too seriously; it may fend off mocking by others, and even prompt positive face-work by them.

Conclusions

This chapter as a whole has analyzed a wide range of humorous exchanges. The investigation of particular joking contexts revealed not just hybrid forms of the traditionally recognized genres, but also varieties of the personal anecdote, jointly produced narratives, and wordplay interaction not previously treated in research on humor. This contextual study of humor illustrates the role of the audience in eliciting, encouraging, interrupting, redirecting, and evaluating the joking performance and emphasizes precisely this performance aspect of most conversational humor. Conversational humor generally allows us to present a personality, share experiences and attitudes, and promote rapport. We integrate our narratives and wordplay into conversation both topically and through audience participation. Joint production and turn taking make these forms far less aggressive than mocking and sarcasm, which attack another person and flout politeness, albeit within a play frame. Punning as a type of wordplay may function either to amuse or to verbally attack. Both types are aggressive in disrupting turn taking and topical talk, and in testing for understanding, but the punning attack adds personal aggression as well. When directed at participants within the group, the more aggressive forms of joking depend on a customary joking relationship developed through a history of interaction: They convey positive politeness or solidarity by flouting negative politeness conventions, and hence show that the relationship need not stand on formalities. At the same time, apparently aggressive conversational joking enhances rapport by demonstrating coparticipation in competitive play on an equal basis. While they cause competition in interaction as a whole, mocking, sarcasm, and irony produce little local effect on the organization of talk; they work more as social control on the recipient than to present a self for the joker.

4

The Metalingual Function of Joking

> It was a kind of code between them, as though recognition depended on insult and invective, affection upon rhetorical display.
>
> Robert Coover, *Pinocchio in Venice* ■

In the preceding chapter, on the interpersonal dimension of conversational humor, we saw that joking could reveal group norms. In poking fun at undesirable behavior patterns of outsiders and lapses among insiders, mocking and sarcasm serve as a control on in-group behavior. Now I would like to investigate the role of joking in circumscribing behavior in the linguistic domain as such, in helping conversationalists evolve a common code and enforcing a way of speaking for the particular interaction, for the group, and, ultimately, for the linguistic community at large. To the degree that joking comments on linguistic form, it counts as "metalingual" in the sense of Jakobson (1960): It allows conversationalists to point out and agree on what is laughable about a turn of phrase or word choice—and hence, it helps them to negotiate the sort of grammar and meaning appropriate to their particular interaction. Though *metalinguistic* has often replaced Jakobson's original term in publications since, I purposely stick to or revert to *metalingual,* since it more readily suggests everyday talk by contrast with formal linguistic description.

Jakobson defines the metalingual function of language as deriving from attention to the code itself, which is to say talk about the forms of talk, say in requests for clarification and explications of word meanings. Jakobson follows Whitehead and Russell (1910–13) and modern logicians generally in drawing a fundamental distinction between two levels of language: so-called "object-language," focused on the world of objects and events (which exhibits Jakobson's referential function), and "metalanguage," focused on language itself; and he makes this distinction just as fundamental as the one between the referential focus and a focus on the speaker's attitude toward the topic (emotive function), or on the reaction of the addressee (conative function), and so on.

Metalingual Joking

Jakobson stresses the "glossing" function of metalingual talk in utterances such as *"flunk* means *fail"* and "A *sophomore* is a *second-year student,"* but he also mentions that any process of language learning, including a child's acquisition of the native tongue, will involve much metalingual talk. So the metalingual function appears clearly when a father reminds a child to say *Sue and I* instead of *me and Sue;* but it looms just as large when the big sister mocks her kid brother for saying *pasketti* instead of *spaghetti.* Not surprisingly, then, at some point in or around adolescence, the children we tutored metalingually turn back around and address their attention—usually sarcastically—to our antiquated speech habits, as we will see in several of the passages cited below. And this mocking of patterns between groups with different ways of speaking leads us to one metalingual dimension of joking.

Further, wordplay can be seen to have a metalingual significance of its own in expressing connections between words usually considered fortuitous by linguists: For example, while Saussure himself (1916:126–27) places similarity of sound image right alongside other "associative" relations, nevertheless he characterizes punning relations as "rare" and "abnormal, for the mind naturally discards associations that becloud the intelligibility of discourse." Still, associative relations based purely on sound similarity are apparently real enough to normal language users, especially those who pun regularly. As the saying goes, "puns are not just some antics." More than just being funny, puns also make us attentive to contextually inappropriate senses of words and to spurious relations in vocabulary. Moreover, as Farb (1973:88) points out rather colorfully, obscene puns subversively undermine the sanctity of taboo words, and find phonological counterparts for them even among more decent lexical items. Derrida (1974:109ff.) goes so far as to suggest that the associative relations of motivation and resemblance between words may be as important a part of the language system as their basic Saussurian dyadic sound/meaning character; and puns work to reveal these interrelations, as Culler (1988:12) argues.

Though the ear [Old English *ere*] as an organ of hearing bears no historical relation to the ear of grain [Old English *ǽre*], a pun like the one in the child's riddle joke below can highlight the closeness of the two in folk etymology. The visually iconic connection between the two real-world objects we associate with the linguistic form *ear* is apparently too salient to ignore so long as they are both tied to a single sequence of sounds and letters.

QUESTION: Why shouldn't you tell secrets in a cornfield?
ANSWER: Because there are ears everywhere.

We talk not only to represent meaning in sound, as the traditional "Message Model of Communication" (see Akmajian et al. 1984) would lead us to believe, but also to enjoy the process itself. Puns turn the process of talk to play. The punning message calls attention to itself; its organization thus illustrates the "poetic" focus, in Jakobson's terms, but its *effect* is metalingual in commenting on the language system. Puns expose the oversimplification inherent in the linear account of language as an arbitrary representation of a single meaning by a single discrete form. As Redfern (1984:9) has it, "Puns illuminate the nature of language in general." Wordplay expresses something *fun*damental about talk and language, and thereby participates in the metalingual function.

Given that we all continue to adjust our ways of speaking to new groups and situations as well as to evolving patterns and vocabulary, we all exhibit certain patterns of speech which will strike some others as funny—both in the sense of 'odd' and in the sense of 'laughable'—to say nothing of careless word choices and clumsy constructions our listeners may interpret in ways that make them comical. For the linguist, this metalingual joking opens a window on the sort of grammar and meaning "emergent" in a particular conversational context, in the sense of Hopper (1988). In parallel fashion, joking about the way outsiders speak with each other, and about their own inept phrasing, provides interlocutors with a key to the sorts of talk appropriate in their particular interaction and group. It should help to clarify the following discussion if we first examine passages where the participants poke fun at language originating outside the group, before turning to metalingual mocking within the group, especially since this latter type can take one of two trajectories: The participants doing the mocking can either confront offending speakers with the linguistic object of their mirth or they can carry on their joking outside their hearing. Obviously the two courses of action have their own separate interactional significance, which will come in for discussion as appropriate.

Mocking Talk from Outside

Participants in talk may have occasion to ridicule forms of language which originate outside their current interaction or outside their group entirely. They may cite the source of the offending discourse, or one participant may just fall into a particular manner of speaking recognizable to the others, as in the passage below, where Leona and Sally conspire to parody current catch phrases about technological innovations. In particular they are joking about the machine they have been asked to put up with so that the student assistant, Tamara, can tape record their conversation. Leona and Sally are two secretaries who work in the same office; and they routinely pepper their talk with all kinds of humor, as examples in previous chapters have demonstrated.

LEONA: It's a good tape recorder. It's a *nice* one, huh?

SALLY: It's a beauty.
LEONA: Beauty. Yes. Top of the line. State of the art.
SALLY: Huh huh [huh.]
LEONA: [And the] cutting edge.
SALLY: *All* of the above.
LEONA: *All* of the above. *Oh.* I *love* it. Can I *have* it huh huh
         heh heh he he [he.]
SALLY: [Huh]huhhuhhuh.
LEONA: It's beautiful, oh my God.

The gushing repetition here suggests that both speakers have adopted a mocking key, in the sense of Hymes (1972), and have consciously expropriated voices not their own and at odds with the actual interaction. The discrepancy between the speakers' own beliefs and their verbal performance creates the script clash characteristic of jokes and joking according to current thinking on humor. The metalingual function of joking in conversation appears here: In holding up questionable talk for ridicule, it helps participants clarify what is acceptable in their own speech, and thereby allows them to achieve interactions in which they "speak the same language," and this fosters rapport. As Ziv (1984:33) maintains, humor opens and enhances interpersonal relations. It provides a test for shared knowledge, and hence proof of group identity, so "humor also creates a common language." An investigation of joking thus provides insight into the sort of grammar and semantics deemed appropriate in a particular conversation and group, and on the process whereby participants negotiate them.

Sally and Leona identify patterns of talk they find worthy of ridicule by playing the role of speakers who talk that way. In the next excerpt, Ned and Lydia poke fun at the language in a text Brandon is reading aloud to them, namely a brochure describing state park facilities. Ned pretends not to understand the contextually more appropriate sense of *covered* in order to pun sarcastically on it, and thus to comment indirectly on the ambiguity of the construction in the brochure. This passage again comes from a set of tapes I have cited in foregoing chapters: Brandon and his family are spending a long weekend at the home

of his parents, Frank and Lydia, along with the family of his
brother Ned.

BRANDON: {reading} Covered picnic tables, er boating.
NED: Like with a tablecloth or what?
LYDIA: He he he.
BRANDON: {reading} Camping [and food]
NED: [Huh huh huh]
LYDIA: [Checkered] che(he)ckered ta-
         (ha)ble cloths hhh.

In both these initial examples, conversationalists conspire to
laugh at patterns of talk which originate outside their current
interaction and group. In parodic presentation of talk associated
with others or in sarcastic punning and comment on its pecu-
liarities, we define by negative example the sort of talk appropriate to our own interactions. Presumably we learn to pay
special attention to those words and constructions we hear held
up for ridicule. Since participants in both excerpts cited target
language from an indefinite or unnamed source, their attention
really focuses on the linguistic forms themselves, and the metalingual function ranks quite high.

Sometimes even a relatively objective descriptive remark about
a linguistic matter can elicit laughter, as in the excerpt below,
again involving the brothers Brandon and Ned, where neither
parody nor punning occurs. Indeed, what Ned points out and
Brandon finds funny is a rather technical observation about English vocabulary, prompted by Ned's difficulty in accessing the
crucial lexical item. Ned has been questioning Brandon about
the autobiography of filmmaker Frank Capra, which Brandon has
been reading.

BRANDON: His early films were made for him. And his later
         films were made-
NED: Name me another early film. (1.5) You just happen.
         to have a,
BRANDON: There's got to be a filmography in here. I would
         th-
NED: *Film*ography. You can't call it a cinematography
         which is what it ought to be called.

BRANDON: Huh heh heh heh. {sniffs}
NED: But they were using that wo(ho)rd (h)already.

Far from mocking a particular speaker, text, or style, then, Ned comments on the code in the narrow sense.

Especially in this last case, but clearly in the preceding examples as well, humorous attention to linguistic form contrasts sharply with the examples of mocking we observed at the end of chapter 3, where something someone says, rather than concern with their way of speaking or with the language itself, provides a motive for a personal attack. When we mock someone for a slip of the tongue, we generally focus on their carelessness or clumsiness and not on the linguistic form they botched. Central to what we called the customary joking relationship was precisely this personal focus vis-à-vis a focus on the materials of humor as such. The two can, of course, become quite difficult to untangle in contexts where certain participants regularly try to make fun of the way others talk—a matter we confront head-on in the following section on mocking present participants for the form of their talk.

Mocking Talk within the Context

Participants may also comment on linguistic patterns and idiosyncracies which originate within their present conversation, though perhaps from speakers representing a different social group. For instance, in the next excerpt, Mary and Amy take their mother, Patricia, to task for what they consider an inappropriate use of the word *Arabian*. Each repeats the offending term with laughter, then Amy mentions camels to clarify the association the girls have for *Arabian*—as opposed, presumably, to *Arab*. Mary recorded this interaction while spending the Thanksgiving break at the home of her mother and father, Patricia and Ralph. Mary's younger sister, Amy, is also home from college for Thanksgiving.

PATRICIA: So an Indian couple come or Arabian or whatever they were.

MARY: He (h)Arabian heh heh heh.
  AMY: Heh heh (h)Ara(ha)bian hehehe. They come in on
          little *ca*mels.
RALPH: Huh [hahaha.]
MARY: [Hehehe.]

Mary and Amy accomplish far more here than just having a little fun at their mother's expense. For one thing, they signal to her that they consider the term *Arabian* odd in this context. At the same time, they band together in solidarity against their mother, and align themselves generally against any who use *Arabian* in the offending way. This allows them to fill in a detail in their strategies for using this particular lexical item, and commits them to being careful with it in the future. In this way, over time, members of a language community and its subgroups come to a fuller picture of the forms of talk appropriate to each sort of interaction.

I would now like to consider in some detail another passage in which Amy and Mary joke about a construction their mother uses, and confront her with it. This time their joking leads to explicit metalingual discussion of the objectionable utterance, involving everyone present.

PATRICIA: {from adjacent room} There's a red pen
               on the couch. Who belongs to it.
AMY, MARY, RALPH: {all giggle}
MARY: Who belongs to the red pen, Mom.
PATRICIA: The kitten's playing with it. She's shoving
               it all over. And if it's open,
AMY: Well I guess the kitten be*longs* to the red
               pen.
MARY: Huh huh hehehe.
PATRICIA: She had it underneath the cushion.
AMY: She still hasn't picked up on it.
MARY: Hehe hahhahhah.
PATRICIA: What am I picking up?
AMY: You said, "Who be*longs* to the red pen."
PATRICIA: That's what I meant. That's what I *meant*
               to say.

> RALPH: Who belongs to the red pen.
> AMY: Don't you want to say, "Who does the red pen be[long *to?*"]
> PATRICIA: [I know, honey.] But I said, "Who belongs to it." I meant to say, "Who belongs to it." I meant it as a *joke.*
> RALPH: Awahhah.

Mary and Amy laugh at their mother for what they think is an error of inattention, which she will be embarrassed about and correct once she becomes aware of it. They seem unfamiliar with the standard jocular pattern *Who belongs to X?* for *Who does X belong to?,* so Patricia ends up explaining to them what she was trying to do—though she does not tell them it is a stock pattern. But in spite of their misinterpretation of the construction, the girls are still involved in mocking someone for the form of her utterance, and, hence, in metalingual joking.

The mocking begins with a fairly straightforward repeat, though the pronoun *it* gets filled in with the appropriate noun phrase. Then Amy produces an exacerbated version of the error with extra stress on *belong.* In her next turn Amy encourages laughter by noting that Patricia *still hasn't picked up on it.* Then she confronts Patricia with the error directly, presumably still expecting her to repent and correct it. But Patricia assures the kids that she purposely produced the offending construction. This leads Ralph to repeat *Who belongs to the red pen* as if testing to find the problem or as if to reinforce its acceptability. He apparently finds nothing amiss, and presumably uses the pattern himself without realizing that it reverses the logical relationship. Amy then presses on to convince her mother that the pattern is backwards, encouraging her to recognize and correct the seeming error. Patricia finally explains that she used the pattern as a humorous form—at which Ralph laughs, more surprised than mirthful.

Significantly, Amy and Mary align themselves together as teenagers against their mother, who represents the ascending generation. Just as in the first two examples where participants aligned themselves together against some outside source, the girls here form a group to poke fun at a linguistic pattern they reject. The construction at issue represents a logical confusion for the girls, while their mother views it as an acceptable jocular pattern. So the issue is not one of standard versus regional dialect or other nonstandard usage, but of one group against the other. Presumably negotiation of appropriate form always begins as an immediate contextual matter, which may then have consequences for other interactions involving the same participants and so on up to the linguistic community as a whole.

It is not at all rare for conversational joking to merge into serious discussion of the topic in question. So it is only natural for joking about ways of speaking to call forth explicit metalingual comment on vocabulary or constructions. In such cases, both the joking and the serious talk allow participants to exchange views on the acceptability of certain words and phrases. At the same time, such passages provide linguists with valuable insight into the negotiation of form and meaning in the concrete conversational context.

By way of summary, this last passage illustrates: (1) repetition used metalingually to identify an apparent error in usage; (2) an exacerbated error of the same type, which represents a second device for metalingual comment; (3) kids aligning themselves against a parent and against a way of speaking they find funny; (4) a fairly lengthy exchange about the offensive pattern, which illustrates explicit metalingual talk.

The first example in this section illustrated metalingual concern with a single word, and the second revolved around a grammatical construction. I would like to turn now to a passage where one participant laughs at another for a particular manner of speaking or rhetorical stance, namely the use of extreme hyperbole. We have seen how conversationalists can use a repeat to point out something funny in the foregoing turn. In the following excerpt, Sandra mockingly repeats the wildly exaggerated dollar value Greg mentions for a shirt in a claim letter he is composing for a business writing class. Sandra and Greg are undergraduate students engaged to be married: This passage was recorded in Greg's car parked outside a drive-in restaurant.

> GREG: Your miracle product. Your miracle detergent, that was supposed to get the stain out, just ate my shirt away, and I now want the money back for my five hundred dollar silk-shirt.

SANDRA: F(h)ive h(h)undred do(ho)llars. huhhuhhuhhuh he-
          hehe.
GREG: Okay, a hundred and fifty.
SANDRA: O(ho)kay hehehe.

Sandra's laughing repeat shows her surprise and disagreement
with the inflated price Greg suggests, and reflects her disapproval
of his habitual tendency toward hyperbole. Of course, Sandra
may be heard as objecting to a regular habit of Greg's rather than
as commenting—metalingually—on a local form of talk, although
the latter necessarily supplies the vehicle for the former. But Greg
immediately admits his exaggeration with *Okay,* then revises his
estimate drastically downward; and this reaction shows that at
least Greg hears Sandra's laughing repeat as an objection to the
hyperbolic form of his utterance, which he can remedy with a
simple reformulation.

In addition to repeating the objectionable words of the foregoing speaker to point out an error, or reanalyzing them to pun,
the second speaker may draw attention to an error or idiosyn-
cracy by producing a similar construction funny in the same
way. In describing some ways to use eggplants once, I announced
that I had prepared *ratatatouille* that very morning. One of my
listeners cut me off to say: *But it had too many syllablebles,*
which excited general laughter from the group. Instead of repeating my slip as such, he invented a parallel word to exemplify
the error and simultaneously poke fun at my mispronunciation.
In placing a second, isomorphic violation beside the first, this
sort of mocking response not only expresses a more general
metalingual comment, but also seems to direct less aggression
at the first speaker by suggesting how easy it is for anyone to
make the sort of error in question.

Even less confrontational than repeating a flawed word or
construction verbatim or producing a parallel error, the recipient
of a humorously fractured utterance may simply laugh, leaving
it up to the other participants to review the turn for themselves
and determine its problematic character. If slips of the tongue,
nonstandard constructions, and logical lapses are inherently
funny, any method of drawing general attention to them can
excite the amusement of others, and incipient laughter can always

serve as a signal of something funny. Furthermore, as we have seen in the foregoing chapters, laughter is ambiguous enough to go off record, in the sense of Brown and Levinson (1978), with criticism of an error. So laughter in response to an utterance may suffice for others—including the speaker—to become aware of some incongruity in it; and the one who laughs need not go "on record" for correcting or mocking the first speaker. This leaves it up to the original speaker or some other participant to produce the metalingual comment proper, if any is to be forthcoming. I cited an appropriate excerpt to illustrate a related point in chapter 2, which I repeat below. The scene includes the recently married couple Vera and Jim, at the home of Pamela and Teddy for dinner, though only Jim and Teddy speak here.

TEDDY: And I say to her, Sara if you could read now. For
         yourself. *You* could read.
JIM: Uh ha ha *ha* hahaha. Ha*ha*ha.
TEDDY: Uhhuh. Which I suppose is almost too obvious even
         to tell a five-year-old.
JIM: Huh huh huh huh huh huh.

Here Jim's laughter tips Teddy off to review his last turn and recognize it as tautological. Teddy responds by humorously critiquing his own construction, which means Jim gets the credit for noticing the purported problem without really committing himself to verbal aggression as such.

We have seen a range of strategies for attracting attention to something funny about foregoing talk in a particular conversation. In all the cases we observed, the participant who initially produced the funny turn also heard the objection to it and had at least an opportunity to respond to the laughter; and in all but the first example, the first speaker took advantage of this opportunity to comment on or correct the passage at issue. In the following section, we will investigate an example where two participants laugh about a seemingly contradictory remark just outside the hearing of the responsible speaker, which has the effect of creating a separate conversation and preventing the culprit from clarifying her utterance or defending herself.

Mocking as Creation of a New Conversation

The foregoing discussion has shown, first, how participants work together to mock the language of an outsider, and, second, how they confront a present person with their humorous objection to a linguistic form or habit. In this section, we will focus on a situation where some participants take the linguistic form of an utterance as an opportunity to initiate a separate conversation beyond the hearing of the speaker who produced the offending utterance. It might initially seem kinder to avoid openly mocking people who use language differently, and rather to giggle about it among ourselves aside from the main conversation. But on the other hand, this nonconfrontational strategy also prevents those individuals from sharing whatever metalingual insight emerges, and precludes their participation in any discussion of the matter. It thus shuts them out as surely as was the anonymous author of the brochure mocked in the second passage cited in this chapter.

Again, in the following example, repetition picks out a laughable portion of the foregoing turn; and again the passage involves the brothers Brandon and Ned, visiting the home of their parents, Lydia and Frank, along with their families. Brandon decontextualizes a sentence addressed to a child in order to bring out its logical absurdity for an audience which does not include the original speaker. In this situation, unembellished verbatim repetition serves the purpose of drawing others' attention to the logical pratfall. Since Brandon delivers the repeat *sotto voce* to his audience, rather than to the original speaker in the next room, he neither sets it off with laughter nor does he contrastively stress the offending words.

> LYDIA: We had such a nice day today, so you hurry and get rested. Because you're going to have a big nice [day tomorrow.]
> BRANDON: [Hurry and] get rested.
> NED: Uh huhhuhhuhhuhhuh hehe
> BRANDON: That's oxymoronic.

NED: Uhhuhhuhhuh. Yeah. Can you imagine the ox?
         hehehe
BRANDON: No. But I've spotted the moron.
NED: I see. Huhhuhhuh. You'd think as dumb as oxes
         are. To call one a moron would be tauto*log*ical.
         Huhhahaheh.

Once Ned shows his appreciation with laughter, Brandon goes
on to comment precisely on the nature of the error. This segues
into some interesting verbal gymnastics, which I discussed in
some detail in chapter 2. Brandon is making a bid to open a
new, separate conversation with his joking repeat. And in this
new conversation, Brandon and Ned take foregoing talk by someone present as cause for joking. They form a little group of their
own within the larger group present, from which they momentarily exclude Lydia, because of her penchant for what they
consider illogical talk. The metalingual function of joking comes
out clearly here, since Brandon and Ned comment explicitly on
the form of talk; moreover, the control function of metalingual
joking appears in its characterization of a particular way of speaking as inappropriate within the ongoing interaction.

Further, the punning which follows Brandon's metalingual
characterization of Lydia's statement suggests a rationale for the
presence of humor in conversation at all, despite its apparent
lack of contextual relevance. The existence, and especially the
persistence, of humor in conversation indicates that it must
appeal to some principle higher than that which mandates relevance to the current information exchange. Punning and banter
are not simply games conversationalists play in lieu of speaking
topically; wordplay renders conversation more pleasant and
enhances rapport, but it also provides conversationalists with an
opportunity to cooperate in creating a particular form of talk
with conventions of its own for the ongoing interaction—and
this, too, must count as metalingual activity in the broad sense.

The pervasiveness of joking in conversation shows that it is
far from being a disruption or a momentary aberration; and the
infectiousness of verbal humor in particular illustrates how wordplay can become a goal in itself. I have suggested, in line with
Lakoff's Rules of Rapport, that conversationalists actively engage

in joking to render interaction more pleasant and conducive to solidarity. Though a second speaker may jokingly repeat a slip in the preceding turn, thus potentially embarrassing and challenging the first speaker to recognize and correct the error, this task is usually easy enough to solve in the given context, so that the first speaker really receives an opportunity to demonstrate membership and to share enjoyment over the jest. In conversational joking, we signal and test for attitudes and membership in groups, at times aligning ourselves with some participants and against others who exhibit language patterns we find inappropriate. Repetition, pretended misunderstanding, and wordplay in joking help identify unacceptable ways of speaking; and they may have metalingual force in commenting on the constructions and vocabulary in foregoing talk. So joking allows participants to define appropriate talk for their conversation, and thus to enhance rapport.

Funny Metalingual Comment

So far in this chapter, we have investigated passages in which conversationalists poke metalingual fun at the language system itself, at a preexistent text, or at talk by the immediately preceding speaker. Of course, we sometimes comment editorially on our own talk in ways that count as metalingual; and such comments may elicit laughter from our listeners as well. Thus in the passage below, Teddy is already in the midst of a sarcastic narrative about an acquaintance who received a large sum of cash from his father to buy a new car, when he pauses to reflect on the proper past tense inflection for the stock phrase *wheel and deal,* which gets a laugh from Jim.

> TEDDY: See what kind of a deal you can make. But I'm only giving you that- *twen*ty *thou*sand dollars. Uhhuhheh. Well, Henry wheeled and dealt. Wheeled and *dealed?*
> JIM: Uh heh heh heh hehe.
> TEDDY: And he did get it for twenty thousand.

Teddy does not simply repeat the binomial phrase with questioning intonation as a listener might have done in order to point out a problem with its form. Instead, he proposes a corrected version of it, thereby showing both that he recognizes some oddity of his initial formulation, and that he knows where the difficulty lies and what to do about it as well. Consequently, the remark does not sound self-deprecatory the way laughing at one's own slip of the tongue might.

In fact, the proposed reformulation shows that Teddy is not really mocking himself so much as he is highlighting a problem he perceives in the language system itself. *Wheeled and dealt* sounds funny, because it loses the parallelism which identifies the phrase as an "irreversible binomial," in the sense of Malkiel (1959); but *wheeled and dealed* sounds just as funny, because it clashes with the usual past tense form for *deal* (see Norrick 1988 for more on the forms of binomials in conversational contexts). Teddy feels caught between conflicting language patterns, and he chooses to comment on the conflict, rather than to let Jim take him to task for an odd-sounding turn of phrase. The result surely illustrates metalingual focus, and Jim's laughter shows it was funny, but it differs in interesting ways from the other examples adduced so far.

Foreign Words and Phrases

A friend of mine I will call Alan immediately reacts to the French phrases *C'est la vie* or *C'est la guerre* by repeating *la vie* or *la guerre* respectively, pretending to have understood *c'est* as the homophonic English imperative *say*. Of course, as Apte (1985) points out, interlingual puns tend to be phonetically imperfect, due to differences in the phonological systems of separate languages; but this fact does not deter determined punsters like Alan any more than imperfect monolingual puns do. This particular stock humorous response to recurrent French phrases in English works in several ways at once. First of all, it represents interlingual punning in equating *c'est* with *say*. Second, it involves some role-play in the pretended misunderstanding. And, third, it seems initially self-deprecatory, in that the role played is one of a boorish person not conversant with even the most standard French

phrases in English. But at the same time, the pretended misinterpretation can be heard as a sarcastic comment on the occur-
rence of these French phrases at all—either their presence in a
special section of the English code or their use by a particular
speaker. So, fourth, Alan's stock responses clearly illustrate metalingual focus.

Clearly, poking fun at a foreign phrase, whether with a stock
punning response or with some other method of eliciting laughter about it, differs radically from making an allusion or telling
a joke which turns on understanding a foreign language. Thus a
person could cite the erudite one-liner *Coito ergo sum* to test
for a knowledge of Latin and/or familiarity with Descartes,
whereas a stock punning reply like *la vie* in response to the
phrase *C'est la vie* mocks another speaker precisely for injecting
a phrase from a foreign language into the conversation. At the
same time, the *la vie* pun parallels the intentional pronunciation
of foreign words and phrases so as to pretend misunderstanding
of them. Thus saying *Harry Verderchi* to take leave as a supposed
mispronunciation of *arrivederci* makes a punning comment on
the use of Italian in much the same way that the stock *la vie*
response comments on the use of French, and it also projects a
negative self-image of a person not conversant with even the
commonest foreign phrases.

Moreover, punning on a stock foreign phrase like *C'est la vie*
apparently differs little from wordplay on any other stock phrase.
For instance, the same Alan mentioned above characteristically
responds to phrases such as *willy-nilly* with the line *Good ol'
Willy. Remember Willy?* After all, this punning response to *willy-
nilly* can be heard as a comment on its archaic or dialect flavor,
just as the response to *C'est la vie* comments on its foreign origin.
In both cases, the second speaker mocks the first one for using
a particular construction somehow marked vis-à-vis his own
system—so the metalingual force remains approximately constant. See Apte (1985) for notes on some interesting intercultural
aspects of interlingual puns.

The Metalingual Function of Humor Versus Metahumor

As we have seen, joking has metalingual function to the degree
that it comments on language forms or ways of speaking. But

conversationalists may also joke about joking itself, commenting on the form, the comic technique, or the quality of jokes and wordplay—and this we may call "metajoking" or "metahumor." Morreall (1983) and Suls (1983) mention metahumor, but they associate it principally with professional comedians like Johnny Carson, who routinely gets bigger laughs from his post-joke comments than from the jokes themselves. Indeed, he sometimes gives the impression of doing admittedly weak material with the express purpose of having something to build his metahumorous comments around. David Letterman is another popular comedian who gets much mileage from facetious comments about his own comedy material. He, too, gives himself plenty of room for metahumor as he tells trite jokes, reads silly lists, sorts through and tears up the cue cards on which his jokes appear.

Metahumor is not limited to professional comedians. Everyday conversation certainly has its share of remarks about jokes and joking which elicit laughter of their own. In chapter 2, we analyzed a passage in which one participant responds to a pun with the line *That's like a blow to the midriff*. This comment targets the quality and effect of the pun and contributes to the overall humor of the exchange, so it counts as metahumor in the relevant sense. Again, in the following chapter, we will see an example of a metahumorous remark about the content of a narrative joke. In general, speakers may comment on unsuccessful jokes of their own in order to get a laugh after all and save themselves further embarrassment. And they may remark on a joke by someone else, perhaps as a put-down, and perhaps simply as a way of joining in the fun of the moment. Both types appear in the passage cited below.

Roslyn has been invited for a going-away dinner at the home of the married couple Nancy and Daniel, before leaving the area for a job at a new university. They are done eating, but the three remain at the dinner table talking about recent developments in their respective disciplines, when Roslyn picks up and puns on the repeated word *novel* from Daniel's floundering monologue about a book. When she receives no reaction, she produces an evaluative *ick* and a short laugh to show she will not insist on the funniness of her own joke. *Yuck*s, groans, and other signs of displeasure or pain are standard means of receiving and commenting on puns by others, and Roslyn simply appropriates such a strategy for metajoking on a pun of her own. When this comment again elicits no laughter, Daniel comments sarcastically *Pun of the week,* which not only provides a clear example of metajoking, but also succeeds in causing Nancy to laugh.

> DANIEL: The novel is about. The novel- the book's about categories.
> ROSLYN: It's really a novel appro(h)oach hh. (1.0) Ick. Hehhe.
> DANIEL: Pun of the week.
> NANCY: Huhhuhhuhhuh
> DANIEL: The book is a, . . .

Sacks (1974) maintains that conversationalists gain points in interaction if they can show they understand a joke someone else makes, but refuse to be amused by it. According to this view of conversation as a competitive enterprise, metajoking is a particularly powerful device for recipients of a joke, since it allows them to demonstrate understanding of the joke and to put it down, while withholding appreciation. At the same time, metahumor supplies a strategy for commenting on our own less than successful attempts at joking in hopes of snatching laughter from the jaws of our listeners or at least saving ourselves some embarrassment.

The Metalingual Function in Everyday Talk

Jakobson's classic treatment of language functions (1960) gives the impression that relatively few utterances exhibit primarily metalingual force. But thirty years of increasingly intense research on naturally occurring conversation have shown that quite a lot of everyday talk is directed at language forms themselves: We are at pains to agree on names and terminology; we work to clarify errors, contradictions, and misunderstandings; we negotiate grammar and meaning, turn-taking and topic choice; we take note of apt phrases and incorporate them into our own talk, while we poke fun at inept phrasing and out-group (nonstandard) forms. Much correction and clarification, as well as apparently frivolous joking, helps us home in on an appropriate register, vocabulary, and grammar.

As pointed out by Jakobson himself, the metalingual focus of language occurs early on with parents correcting children from the time they begin to produce even approximately adultlike utterances. Then the older kids begin correcting and laughing at younger ones. The earliest corrective and mocking exchange I have on tape involves my son, Nick, just three weeks before his fifth birthday, and his little sister, Corinna (Coco), at three years, three months. Nick had just started correcting his sister's talk about two weeks earlier, but he had not yet laughed about the errors or teased her for them in my hearing. The children are growing up bilingual in German and English, and the following exchange took place in German, though the grammatical point involved and the comments on it have exact parallels with cognate words in English: I give first the transcription of the actual German recording, then a close translation, punctuated as if the exchange had actually transpired in English. Nick first corrects what he perceives to be an error by Coco without laughter, then giggles at her second error and explains his amusement in an aside to me—essentially the same way Brandon points out the alleged oxymoron in Lydia's *Hurry up and get rested* in the example cited early on in this chapter.

NICK: Daddy, Coco hat gesagt *gü*ter. Das kann man nicht sagen, oder?
DADDY: Nee, was muß man sagen.
NICK: Coco meint *bes*ser.
COCO: Nein, *gü*ter.
NICK: Nein, Coco, *bes*ser. Du mußt *bes*ser sagen.
COCO: Laß mich, das ich sage.
NICK: ki hi hi. Jetzt hat Coco wieder Unsinn gesagt.

Translation:

NICK: Daddy, Coco just said *good*er. You can't say that, can you?
NEAL: No, what do you have to say.
NICK: Coco means *bet*ter.

COCO: No, *good*er.
NICK: No, Coco, *bet*ter. You have to say *bet*ter.
COCO: Let me that I say.
NICK: ke he he. Coco just said nonsense again.

It may be significant that Nick has come to me with a question about a language form in the first place, and that he is in the midst of a corrective sequence with Coco. So a metalingual frame is already in force; then coming off approval from me, Nick is especially prepared to find infelicities in his sister's talk. In any case, the excerpt provides a good example of how preschoolers talk about language forms, and how they can joke about inappropriate talk. Nevertheless, I cite this example not primarily to demonstrate evolving metalingual awareness or talk about talk among preschoolers, but rather to illustrate the intimate connection between metalingual comment and joking at this early age.

Conclusions

I hope this chapter gives some idea of the metalingual import of conversational joking. Metalingual joking represents the social control function of humor focused on the form of talk. We have seen how joking can provide a window on the grammar and meaning emergent in the concrete conversational context. The examples adduced illustrate the range of strategies we use for pointing out errors, how we realign the participants in a conversation to test for membership and attitudes toward the form of talk. Even metalingual remarks about incongruities in the language system may elicit laughter. Joking about the form or use of foreign words and phrases does not differ significantly from joking about any other linguistic matter which departs from some norm. Metalingual joking ultimately targets questionable talk rather than the errant speaker as such, though the one who produces a laughable utterance attempts to explain or correct it where possible. Our apparently frivolous joking about ways of speaking helps us define the sorts of talk appropriate to our interaction, which, in turn, lets us feel we "speak the same language" and fosters rapport. Wordplay makes us attentive to aspects of our vocabulary usually considered spurious and beyond the purview of linguistic description, so it expresses metalingual focus of a special kind. Attention to the form of talk itself is neither a rare nor an erudite activity: Many utterances in everyday talk have metalingual force, and joking ranges among the most important.

5

Telling Jokes

PERFORMANCE, TEST, MUTUAL REVELATION

> But the teller of the comic story tells you beforehand
> that it is one of the funniest things he has ever heard,
> then tells it with eager delight, and is the first person
> to laugh when he gets through. And sometimes, if he
> has had good success, he is so glad and happy that
> he will repeat the 'nub' of it and glance around from
> face to face, collecting applause, and then repeat it
> again. It is a pathetic thing to see.
>
> Mark Twain, "How to tell a story" ■

In foregoing discussions we have had occasion to touch on various aspects of joke telling in conversation—its integration into the overall organization, how it enhances rapport in helping conversationalists identify common group memberships and shared ways of speaking, but this chapter will focus on joke telling as performance, test, and mutual revelation.

Joke Telling as an Interactional Achievement

In this first section, I will try to develop an interactional account of joke telling in conversation which builds primarily on work by Sacks and Sherzer. Sacks (1974) analyzed a dirty joke in conversation, concentrating on the organization of the telling, and noted a test function for jokes: The speaker demonstrates knowledge and challenges hearers to prove they understand by laughing at the proper place. Legman had earlier (1968) suggested that the teller of a dirty joke directs aggression at listeners in exposing them to its offensive subject matter. The teller thus tests not only for understanding but also for a kind of guilty complicity in the sexual or scatalogical scene the joke portrays. And while this makes dirty jokes more aggressive, it makes them more conducive to the creation of conversational involvement at the same time.

Sherzer (1985) goes beyond Sacks in identifying a twofold aggression in jokes: against the hearer, who is subjected to a little intelligence test, and against the butt of the joke—perhaps a person or group the teller and hearer conspire to laugh at. I follow Sacks, Legman, and Sherzer in recognizing both aggression and a test element in jokes and joking, but I insist that both the teller and the hearer learn something about each other, and I stress that the test routinely aims to find common ground, rather than to embarrass the hearer. Thus we would be more likely to quote *Cogito ergo consum* to a colleague familiar with Descartes, in a spirit of sharing, than as a put-down to someone we expected to know no Latin. It is up to the joker to signal the play frame and to express the jest in a form accessible to members of a certain group, and it is up to the listener to interpret and then reinterpret the turn to get the joke, and to show understanding with laughter. If the two coordinate their timing, they both share in the payoff of amusement and increased rapport.

Tannen (1984) argues that humor makes a person's presence in a conversation more strongly felt than other sorts of contributions. According to Goffman (1967), we interact to present a self, to gain knowledge of others, and to enhance self-image for ourselves and others, so telling jokes should provide an opportunity for the joker to gain credit for a performance *and* to "gather relevant social data" about the audience—data on beliefs, attitudes, group membership, and so on. Since jokes often trade on personal problems or slips and socially sensitive topics such as ethnic identity, politics, and sex, they allow the joker to demonstrate a certain tolerance and/or insensitivity, while offering hearers a chance to signal their agreement, shock, resentment, or what have you. So jokes help us get to know each other, and to signal rapport, where appropriate. If joke telling works to present a self and to gauge the attitudes of others, then we can maintain the notion of jokes as tests without overstating their aggression toward the hearer. In addition, since jokes allow us to direct aggression at a third party, they can help create and enhance feelings of rapport. When group members express aggression against outsiders, they do so within the group as a show of solidarity, rather than as an open challenge to the non-members, according to Apte (1987) and Schutz (1989). Joking ends up more a matter of group cohesion than testing; and even the testing serves as a control on what sorts of talk and behavior are acceptable to participants in the interaction.

In analyzing the telling of a dirty joke among adolescent boys, Sacks (1974) concluded that "jokes, and dirty jokes in particular, are constructed as 'understanding tests'" (1974:346). He stressed that jokes differ from other stories in calling for laughter immediately upon completion. So they test the hearers' background knowledge, their ability to get the joke, and their sangfroid in the face of the joke's potentially offensive subject matter, in the sense of Legman (1968). But knowledge in sexual matters is at a premium among adolescents, which naturally accentuated the test function of joking in Sacks's example. Prefabricated jokes provide adolescents with a serviceable means of presenting the knowledge they have (or are beginning to acquire), and of testing for this knowledge among their compatriots. The teller demonstrates knowledge of the joke's matter and more or less dexterity in performing the text, while the audience demonstrates with laughter the ability to access the necessary background information and to hook it up with the current discourse in a new way to get the joke. As Sacks points out, the audience may groan sarcastically or produce mirthless laughter at the appropriate juncture to show understanding while withholding appreciation, and they may even interrupt at specific points if they already know the joke. This complementary exhibition of shared knowledge, particularly when it involves some specialized or arcane source, attests to common interests and encourages mutual involvement.

But surely adults do not usually feel the need to test each other's knowledge of sexual lore, though they may well want to test others' attitudes about sex, seeking the limits of their permissiveness, the threshold of their taboo areas. Joke telling allows conversationalists to demonstrate and test for all sorts of shared knowledge and attitudes, which may or may not involve sexual scripts. And the tests we pose in telling jokes seek not primarily to embarrass hearers, but rather to give them an opportunity to affirm shared knowledge and beliefs. In fact, it is common for the joke teller to fill the audience in on any background knowledge they may lack in the interest of ensuring their understanding and enjoyment, and hence the success of the performance. Brandon does just this in the following excerpt, before producing the actual joke text. Brandon and Ned are discussing their plans for the coming weekend, when a name makes a joke topically relevant for Brandon, and he insists on telling it before continuing with serious topical talk. The passage derives from a set of tapes I cited often in the preceding chapters: Ned and Brandon are brothers spending a long weekend at the home of their parents, Frank and Lydia, along with their respective families.

BRANDON: Then they were going to go see Dwight Yoakum and Pol- Dolly Parton?

NED: And Clint Black.

BRANDON: Oh I've got a joke for you.

NED: You probably don't know Clint Black.

BRANDON: I don't. I've got a joke for you. You know who Red *A*dair is? Red *A*dair? He's the guy who goes around and puts out *oil* well fires?

NED: Yeah.

BRANDON: Okay. He's coming back from Indonesia. He's been over there a while putting out fires. And he stops off in Las Vegas. On his way back to Houston. He sits down at the bar next to a guy and he starts up a conversation and the guy starts talking about what a ter*ri*fic town Las Vegas is. He says, "Not only is there gambling and good golf and *all* this stuff but the entertainment here is just spectacular. Two nights ago I saw the greatest song-and-dance man ever. Lenny Davis Jr. And this guy was terrific.

He's very old at this point but- boy he can still hoof."

And Red Adair looks at the guy and says, "*Len*ny Davis Jr. You mean *Sam*my Davis Jr."

NED: Huh huh huh.

BRANDON: "Sammy, Lenny, I don't know. But the guy was great. I tell you the entertainment here is terrific." And he says, "And *last* night. You know who I went to see? I saw the *best* country and western singer I've seen in my *life*. This gal was just terrific. Sings like an angel. Molly Parton."

And Red Adair looks at the guy. "*Mol*ly Parton. Everybody knows that it's *Dol*ly Parton. How can you call *Dol*ly Parton *Mol*ly Parton."

So their talk goes a little further and the guy says, "By the *way, you* look familiar to me. Who are you?"

And he says "Oh I'm Red A*dair.*"

And he says "Oh are you still sleeping around with Ginger *Rog*ers?"

NED: Uh*huh* huh huh huh *huh* huh huh. Uh huh *hah*. That's pretty cute.

BRANDON: *I* liked it.

NED: But it doesn't have anything to do with Dwight Yoakum.

BRANDON: No. But Dolly *Par*ton is [what-]

NED: [Oh. Dolly] *Par*ton. And you don't *know* Clint Black.

BRANDON: is what rang the bell.

NED: Clint Black is . . .

This passage illustrates a number of interesting points, which receive further attention below, but of primary importance here is Brandon's concern that Ned possesses crucial background information before Brandon goes into the joke itself. After interrupting the original discussion with *I've got a joke for you,* then cutting off Ned's attempted return to the topic with a terse *I don't* and a repetition of the announcement of a coming joke, Brandon first asks whether Ned knows the central character in

the joke. Only when Ned responds positively does Brandon signal the beginning of the joke proper with *okay*. Far from testing
for this background information, Brandon wants to ensure that
Ned is prepared to understand the joke and thus appreciate the
performance.

The primary interactional point of telling a joke then comes
closer to performance and entertainment than to testing. The
performance allows the teller to present a self for ratification by
the audience, in the sense of Goffman. And even when testing
is a goal of the performance, the test seems geared to gathering
interpersonal data, again in Goffman's sense. Telling jokes as
performance and testing for interpersonal information ends up
as a strategy for "mutual revelation," as described by Tannen
(1989). It leads to solidarity precisely because the teller demonstrates attitudes and membership in groups, while giving the
audience a chance to pass a test to show shared background
knowledge and group affiliation. Hence joke telling counts as
positive politeness in the sense of Lakoff (1973) and Brown and
Levinson (1978), as an invitation to demonstrate membership
and solidarity.

Sherzer (1985:219) relates the test function of jokes to their
aggressive character. He distinguishes two potential victims of a
joke's telling: the victims named in the joke text, and "the listeners who are suddenly being given a short intelligence test and
being forced, whether they want to or not, to publicly display
knowledge or lack of knowledge about a particular area, perhaps
taboo." Still, the aggression most speakers direct at their listeners
in telling them jokes cannot rate very high on the scale of aggressive acts. Even an erudite allusion joke like *Though William shake
his spear, Anne hath a way* most likely appears in conversation
between literary-minded cognoscenti as a show of shared knowledge, rather than to test someone's doubtful background in
Shakespeare by way of aggression. If anything is being tested in
such cases, it is presumably the audience's willingness to laugh
about the subject matter in question. And, as the Red Adair joke
above illustrates, the teller, out of self-interest, in hopes of a well-
received performance, may even check in advance to ensure that
the audience possesses all the necessary background information.

Moreover, the audience submits voluntarily to the aggression and testing of the joke, and helps determine the shape it takes. In recent years, it has become increasingly clear that the audience acts as coauthor of any text (see Duranti 1986 and references there). This holds especially true of narratives, which listeners must interpret and act on in ways which take all kinds of contextual, personal, and social factors into account; for relevant data and analyses, see Sharrock and Turner (1978), Polanyi (1979), Goodwin (1986), and Spielman (1987). Narratives characteristically make further talk about their content topically appropriate upon completion. This means recipients routinely formulate or reinterpret the point of the story and/or comment evaluatively on it so as to relate it to a following narrative or other topical concerns in their ongoing talk; Ryave (1978) and Jefferson (1978) give convincing examples of this. More than anyone else, Schegloff has demonstrated repeatedly the interactional, interdependent character of talk in interaction. Any stretch of talk in face-to-face interaction represents a mutually negotiated product, and this certainly obtains for any performance of conversational humor (see Schegloff 1982; 1987; 1988 among others). But even Freud (1905:105) stressed the crucial role of the audience for verbal humor, writing that only what the listener allows to be a joke *is* a joke—otherwise it is simply a story, perhaps humorous, perhaps not.

Thus when Brandon announces for the first time *I've got a joke for you* in the excerpt above, Ned ignores him and asserts his interest in the current topic with *You probably don't know Clint Black,* and he could just as well reassert his own topic after Brandon repeats his offer to tell a joke. He could then also refuse to listen to the questions Brandon asks about Red Adair, or he could answer in the negative instead of responding *Yeah,* which finally sets the stage for the joke performance. Even then, Ned could get up and leave or verbally interrupt Brandon's performance to show disinterest; nevertheless Ned ends up not just listening but even producing appreciative laughter near the middle of the joke to signal interested listenership. In short, Ned hardly acts like someone preparing for aggression or a testing which will put him on the spot. Like Ned, we typically have any number of opportunities to avoid the test and aggression that a joke in conversation entails, but we generally submit ourselves to them gladly, because we hope to share in the payoff of entertainment and enhanced rapport with the teller once we laughingly pass the so-called test. We thereby become coconspirators with the joke-teller in our mutual best interest, which certainly seems to diminish any real aggression and to defuse any real test imposed.

As I argued previously, sarcasm and mocking, to name only two sorts of spontaneous conversational joking, express more aggression toward hearers than do canned jokes which only test their understanding. If we view jokes as preformed interactional units for presenting self and gauging the feelings of others, then we can continue to recognize their test function, albeit in a less aggressive form and by way of an exchange of social data. Whatever aggressive component individual jokes may direct toward the audience, conversational humor generally seems to count as a good-natured event keyed to play rather than aggression among adults in our culture.

This interactional view of humor as mutual revelation goes beyond speaker-based approaches, which focus on the teller's knowledge and skill or on the joke as a special type of speech act or a behavioristic stimulus constructed by the performer. And it goes beyond hearer-based approaches, which focus on the audience's ability to decode a message and identify its sources in other discourses or on the joke as a text for deconstruction or a behavioristic response of laughter. It also goes beyond viewing jokes as a teller's aggression against an unwilling listener (Legman 1968), or as tests of understanding (Sacks 1974) or tests of intelligence and knowledge (Sherzer 1985), first in insisting that both the performer and the audience receive new information about each other, and second in stressing that the testing aims to determine or affirm common ground in the form of shared knowledge, beliefs, and attitudes, rather than to show up the audience or to prove the teller's superiority. In many contexts where the participants already know each other quite well, joke telling looks far more like performance for mutual entertainment than any sort of testing beyond simply affirming membership in a common group. In the remainder of this chapter, I hope to demonstrate in some detail just how conversationalists present a self and feel out their audience while performing narrative jokes.

Narrative Jokes in Conversation

In the long excerpt below where a single participant tells three jokes in a row to the assembled members of his extended family, no testing need be done to determine membership or understanding, so the teller seems primarily to be performing for the sake of entertaining his audience. I cite the whole passage as a unit to give some feeling for the development of a joke-telling session: how a play frame is established, how something in that play frame then suggests a joke on the current topic, and how one joke leads to another. In this particular case, the participants maintain the play frame for about twenty-five turns of teasing and banter, and the first, topically appropriate joke leads into two further jokes, before the tape ends. This pattern closely parallels other series of narrative jokes in my data where participants take turns telling jokes: I chose this series with a single, rather accomplished teller to make the passage as a whole easier to follow. Again the joke-teller is Brandon, familiar from the initial passage in this chapter where he told a joke about Red Adair. He and Ned are brothers, sons of Frank and Lydia, whose home they are visiting along with their own families for an extended weekend. Sherry is married to Brandon, and Claire to Ned. Together they are trying to work out the logistics of preparing themselves and four small children for an early departure the next morning.

> SHERRY: Mom was saying someone should shower *now*. And I said I want to do my hair in the morning. I don't want to do it now.
> NED: I don't look good if I shower now.
> BRANDON: Huh huh huh huh. You're right.
> NED: *Heh* heh. *Heh* heh. Huh huh huh.
> BRANDON: Haw (h)or any other time for that matter. [huh huh huh huh huh.]
> LYDIA: [*Heh* heh heh heh heh.]
> NED: Hahaha. Let me rephrase.
> LYDIA: I don't care if you're-
> NED: *Let* me re*phrase.* Hehhehhehheh.

BRANDON: Well if-

LYDIA: I'm running the dishwasher right now so you'll all have hot water in the morning.

BRANDON: If someone wants to be pushy about it I-

NED: That's not the way it [works in *my* house.]

BRANDON: [I could take a shower] right now.

LYDIA: Are you going to [be pushy about it] or,

BRANDON: [and have it out of] the way.

CLAIRE: And you would still look good tomorrow?

BRANDON: {self-assuredly} Hey.

NED: If we just [take *shor*tish showers.]

SHERRY: [If we take enough] of that sunscreen along with us and rub it on anywhere it looks-

BRANDON: Huh huh it looks ridiculous.

NED: But it *works,* [right?]

BRANDON: [huh huh] huh.

NED: And you stop looking ridiculous. You look like you've got [a lot of *sun* cream on.]

BRANDON: [Huh huh huh.]

NED: Heh heh heh heh. Hey (h)look (h)at the good looking *guy* comple(he)tely co(ho)vered huh huh huh. (huhh)with su(hu)n cream. hhhh.

BRANDON: Huh huh huh. That's a good-looking pile of cream over there.

NED: U*huh* huh huh huh.

BRANDON: Eehehehehehe. Look at that *poor* man. *Yeah* but look at his *suit.* Heh heh {inhales}, You know that joke?

NED: I don't think I know it. Is that all the joke?

BRANDON: No. A guy comes *in.* Says, "I need a *suit."* Guy says, "I've got the perfect suit for you." He puts the *pants* on. He says, "One of these legs is four inches longer than the other." He says, "That's okay just hold it up like this when you walk" and he puts on the *coat.* And the *sleeves* are too long.

NED: I *have* heard this joke. Huh huh.
        {Ned and Lydia laughing passim to end}

BRANDON: He says, "Tuck it under." He takes it, goes out.

"Hey *poor* man but what a *nice suit.*"

NED: Huh huh huh ho. I've heard that joke before but I've never heard it done like *that.*

FRANK: I didn't hear a word of it. I don't know wh-

NED: Huh *huh.* It doesn't matter. It's a *great* joke. Ah. Ah.

LYDIA: I think you and Dad should take baths to*night,* and let those *oth*er people take showers in the morning.

NED: To*geth*er. Very very g- y'know good joke.

BRANDON: It's one of the great ones.

NED: It's right up there with, (1.0)

SHERRY: Did he tell you his Harvard joke?

BRANDON: Oh yeah. That's a good joke.

NED: You can't tell that *here.*

BRANDON: No. This one's-

NED: Oh. *Dif*ferent Harvard joke.

BRANDON: This one's fine.

NED: Heh huh huh huh. I only know two. And they're both dirty.

SHERRY: This isn't.

BRANDON: This is a pretty good one. This is a pretty good one. Uh Oregon- Oregon boy goes to *Har*vard. And he's just a young kid y'know? Ready to start his freshman year and he's kind of intimidated. He goes out into Harvard *Yard* for the first time. And his instructions are that he's supposed to meet at the library at such and such a time and he's looking around the yard and there's *all* the ivy-covered buildings and they all look the same to him and he sees a guy walking the other direction and he's a slightly older guy with a *big* Harvard letter sweater on. Obviously a Harvard student. So he goes up to the fellow and says, "Can you tell me where the library's *at?*" And the fellow looks at him and says, (4.0) "*I* am a *Har*vard student. We're standing here in *Har*vard Yard. I as*sume* at some point in your life you're going to be a Harvard student too. And the first thing you should *know.*

Is that no *Harv*ard student ends his sentences with
a preposition. So *no* I do *not* know where the
library's *at.*

LYDIA: Huh *bah* [hah hah. Isn't that cute?]

FRANK: [Huh huh huh huh huh.]

BRANDON: And the fellow thinks for a second. And he says,
(1.0) "Okay. Uh can you tell me where the library's
at *ass*hole." {sniffs}

FRANK: Oh. Huh heh.

NED: See [I view that as dirty.]

BRANDON: [huh heh heh heh.]

NED: And I know that I'm a prude about these things
but still. I think it's something about that last *word.*

BRANDON: Sorry.

NED: It *is* the joke I know. It's okay. It's a pretty good
joke.

LYDIA: It's a *funny* joke.

FRANK: It doesn't end in a preposition.

NED: No.

SHERRY: Hheh.

FRANK: He accomplished his goal.

LYDIA: It's very funny.

NED: Oh it all *works.* I was just kind of surprised that
it ended up being the same joke I knew.

BRANDON: Then there's the other one where-

NED: which I viewed as dirty. Whereas yours of course
isn't.

BRANDON: No see when I-

NED: Nothing dirty about assholes.

BRANDON: think of dirty I think of scatological. Not just the
fact that there happens to-

NED: Nothing scatological about assholes, no.

BRANDON: to be a four-letter word in it.

FRANK: Huh huh huh huh huh huh.

NED: Huhhuhhuhhuh. What could be scatological about
an asshole.

BRANDON: Well I think of that word in a more generic sense.

NED: Ahha.

LYDIA: So what's the other one.

BRANDON: An*oth*er one there's [two guys on the plane.]

NED: [I don't think I *get* it.] Huh huhhuh.

BRANDON: And they're talking for a little while and finally the one guy turns to the other one and says, "You're a Harvard grad aren't you." And the other fellow says "Yeah. As a matter of fact I *am*. How'd you know?" And he says, "There was a certain something about the *cut* of your clothes the air that you carried yourself with. Just sort of the savoir faire that you had. I just knew that you were from Harvard." Guy says, "You know that's very observant of you. Particularly for a University of Georgia grad."

LYDIA: [Heh *ha* ha.]

FRANK: [Huh huh huh.]

NED: Uh huh huh.

BRANDON: And the fellow says, "How did you know I was from the University of *Geor*gia." And he says, "Aw I noticed your class ring when you were picking your *nose.*"

NED: Heh huh [*huh.*]

LYDIA: [Eh aw.]

FRANK: [He he he] he he hehe.

LYDIA: Isn't that *ter*rible. Oh that's ugly.

FRANK: [Ho ho ho ho ho ho ho.]

BRANDON: [Huh huh huh huh huh huh huh.]

LYDIA: Now see I think that's a worse joke-

BRANDON: I think that's a much dirtier joke [personally.]

LYDIA: [than the-] one with the dirty *word*. Because it's *ug*ly. Y'know. It's low class [compared with the other.]

NED: [And we use] the word *dirty* {tape ends}

To begin with a few remarks on the overall organization of this passage, we should note that the first joke adheres to the topic of the ongoing talk about tomorrow's plans, a topic which has already deteriorated into joking about covering up with sun cream. Brandon uses the punch line from a joke he initially assumes to be familiar to the others. When no one reacts with laughter, he asks *You know that joke?* This counts as the "preface" to a joke-telling, according to Sacks (1974), and it appeals to listeners for some kind of response. Since Ned appears unfamiliar with it, and even asks if the punch line is the whole joke, Brandon feels entitled to move right into his performance.

After a few comments on the first joke by Brandon and Ned, Sherry asks whether Brandon has told his Harvard joke. As pointed out in chapter 2, the telling of one joke by itself makes any other joke topically relevant. Sherry's question again counts as a preface to a joke-telling in Sacks's sense, even though initiated by someone besides the teller. And Ned appropriately responds in the next slot by questioning the tellability of the presumed joke, since he feels it may be too dirty in the current configuration of participants. At the same time, Ned goes on record as familiar with the announced joke or a similar one. Brandon and Sherry assure him that it is a fine joke to tell, and Brandon proceeds to deliver the joke itself. It turns out to be the joke Ned thought was too dirty to tell after all, and this leads to further talk about dirtiness in jokes.

Lydia puts an end to the discussion of the second joke by asking *So what's the other one?* It was Ned who said he knew two Harvard jokes, so Lydia presumably addresses him, but before Ned replies, Brandon launches into his third narrative joke. And this leads back into the discussion of what counts as dirty in jokes when the tape ends. The talk could continue relevantly on this topic or revert to the original topic of tomorrow's plans, but, as we have seen, the telling of one joke makes the telling of further jokes relevant as well. So all three jokes are topically relevant in one way or another: The first grows out of a topical allusion, and it suggests another topically unrelated joke, which, in turn, starts a discussion leading to the telling of a third joke; the second two jokes not only share a reference to Harvard, but also fit cohesively into the whole discussion of dirtiness in jokes.

We have seen how conversationalists jointly negotiate a joke-telling session. Tellers may announce their own jokes, as Brandon does in the first case; or another participant may do it for them, as when Sherry asks if Brandon has told the Harvard joke or when Lydia asks what the other one was. But either way, the preface to the joke seeks to connect it with the current context (Brandon's *You know that joke?*), while giving other participants a chance to block the performance by saying they do know it. In addition, the others can object to a joke on the grounds that it may be inappropriate (Ned's *You can't tell that here*), though ensuing discussion can clear the way for telling after all, as happens in the passage above. Then the listeners must cede their right to speak in turn, while the teller attempts to produce an entertaining performance; still, listeners may interrupt briefly with appreciative laughter or to say they recognize the joke after all, as we also see in each joke above. Finally, the listeners routinely respond at the correct juncture with laughter, often followed by comments of various kinds on the joke, the performance, and so on. I would now like to go into the matters of teller performance and audience reception in somewhat more detail.

The Joke Performance

The performance aspect of joke telling comes out clearly in the first, *nice suit* joke. Much of its humor depends on the final image of the customer standing on one foot, holding up one pant leg, and retracting one arm to make the suit appear to fit— thereby making himself look ridiculous, and inviting the comment on the poor man with the nice suit. A good joke-teller portrays the man and the situation to heighten the effect of this image. Though Ned does recall the joke part way through the telling, as he interrupts to announce with *I have heard this joke,* he thoroughly enjoys Brandon's performance of it, and compliments him saying *I've heard that joke before but I've never heard it done like that.* Obviously, then, the teller can gain credit through performance even of a joke already familiar to the audience. According to La Fave, Haddad, and Maesen (1976), "There are no jokes"—it is the performance within a concrete context which makes a story funny. The same attitude finds expression in our folklore concerning jokes as well, namely: "Some people can tell 'em and some can't." And despite the overstatement in both versions, they both make an important point, especially from a methodological point of view for the investigation of humor in discourse: Jokes and joking represent performed chunks of talk, which we must study in their natural contexts to fully appreciate.

In this same vein, notice that Brandon manages to elicit appreciative interruptive laughter within the body of each joke he tells. Even if jokes are constructed as understanding tests in the sense of Sacks, clearly they create amusement beyond what their official punch lines call forth. Brandon's physical demonstration of the man with the ill-fitting suit in the first joke caused enough advance laughter to drown the punch line out almost. However, the punch line received advanced billing in Brandon's preface to the joke, and Ned seems to recall the joke in any case, so the actual delivery of the punch line in the final position has lost much of its surprise value: Brandon wisely goes with the flow of the already substantial laughter, tossing the punch line off without overly much ado.

Again, in the next joke, Brandon's portrayal of the overbearing Harvard man in his deprecating attention to prepositions elicits significantly more laughter than the actual punch line. Indeed, the delivery of this exaggerated objection to final prepositions elicits the sort of laughter from Lydia and Frank we would expect from the punch line itself—and they may have heard it as such. In the second Harvard joke, as well as in the Red Adair joke cited earlier, Brandon's performance gets his audience laughing before anything understandable as a punch line falls. Under normal circumstances, an audience already amused by the performance in the buildup of a joke is likely to laugh more at the punch line. Moreover, the total effect of the performance on the audience increases if the buildup also provides a laugh. This demonstrates not only the significance of the performance in a successful instance of joke telling, but also the way jokes entertain the audience in ways unrelated to passing the understanding test enforced by their punch lines.

Another aspect of individual performance in joke telling appears in Brandon's choice of Oregon as the home of the boy who goes to Harvard. Tellers routinely modify this joke text to match the place of telling or their place of residence: Sentence-final prepositions are hardly a regional marker in American speech. So the place chosen as the boy's home offers the teller a chance to personalize the performance and to steer the attitude of the audience to some degree, though the snotty Harvard man remains the final butt of the joke in all the versions I have heard. Brandon moved to Oregon a year prior to this recording, and he may have originally heard this joke told with an Oregon boy as the new Harvard student, but the preceding *uh* and his cutoff and repetition of *Oregon* makes it look like an editing decision Brandon makes on the spot. Either way, it indicates that the teller must make decisions about the presentation of the joke text itself, to say nothing of decisions about voice shifts, gestures, dramatization, and the like, all of which may vary from one telling to the next.

This last point leads to a clearer perception of the joke performance as self-revelation. The teller of a joke presents a self or line, in the sense of Goffman, in several ways. First, the bare distinction between conversationalists who tell jokes and others who do not yields relevant personal data. We all know a person who has "got a million of 'em" and others who claim they simply cannot remember a joke to save their soul. Precisely because joke telling counts as a performance, an extended occupation of the conversational floor with the intention of entertaining the other participants, some speakers revel in joke telling, while others avoid it. Speakers who routinely tell narrative jokes and weave spontaneous wit freely into their talk may pass for scintillating conversationalists with some, while others may consider them frivolous or overbearing.

Second, the decision to tell a joke right here, right now in an ongoing conversation shows the teller has no compunction about derailing the interaction in progress for the ostensible purpose of amusement. Just because a particular event or topic of conversation "reminds me of a joke," it does not mean I must announce the fact and interrupt the regular course of talk to tell it. Tannen (1984) says humor makes a person's presence more strongly felt in a multiparty conversation, and performing jokes well certainly rates even higher than spontaneous humor—again because it involves a performance which suspends the usual give-

and-take of everyday talk. The more serious or important the occasion is for the other participants, the more a joke performance may seem like an intrusion. And the joke-teller risks not only the perception of intruding, but also a potential loss of face if the other participants refuse to listen because they know the joke or if the performance turns out unsuccessful. So when conversationalists announce jokes, they have already revealed a lot about themselves before they even get into the performance proper.

Third, of course, the choice of joke materials strongly reflects the personality of the presenter. Some conversationalists apparently expect a joke to bear contextual relevance, and they may judge negatively the logic and consistency of someone who tells a joke with no obvious topical point, as we see from Ned's question about the connection with Dwight Yoakum after Brandon tells the Red Adair joke in the earlier, shorter passage above. Many of us place a premium on originality in humor, so we tend to rate old jokes low on the scale of laughability and those who tell them low on the scale of social skills; we may even interrupt the telling of a joke we know, as Ned does during the *nice suit* joke, although his final assessment of the performance remains very positive.

If, as Freud (1905) suggests, joking provides a socially acceptable way of venting unconscious emotions, then the topics we choose to joke about suggest something about the feelings we suppress. Consequently, we tend to assume that the teller of any joke which targets a specific professional, ethnic, or religious group accepts some of the negative stereotypes associated with the group. Thus, in his two Harvard jokes, Brandon manages to express aggression against residents of Oregon and students at both Harvard and the University of Georgia. A teller of too many aggressive jokes may come to appear bitter and vindictive. Further, as mentioned above, telling dirty jokes allows adolescents to suggest that they possess sexual lore they only dimly understand. And, of course, the joke-teller may also present a personality conversant with intellectual and arcane subject matter, with the personalities currently popular in the media and so on. The materials of our humor, then, help us present a self for ratification by our audience.

Fourth, the performance of a joke itself reveals a particular personality. We expect the teller to present the buildup clearly and coherently, and to deliver the punch line without telegraphing it in advance. The careful joke performer never laughs till the hearers are also laughing. Failure in any of these departments can *blow the joke,* in the sense of Hockett (1960). "Some people just don't know how to tell 'em," as the traditional wisdom has it; and, of course, much more goes into a really good performance than simply recalling and repeating a joke text from an earlier conversation. We noted in relation to the *nice suit* and Harvard jokes certain strategies Brandon employed to personalize his performance and to enhance its entertainment value. Voice changes, gestures, dramatization, pacing, rhetorical pauses—all these and more—work in concert not only to enliven the performance of a joke, but also to characterize the teller as a person. These same performance factors help determine the amount of aggression a joke expresses toward its butt as well. Our perception of the *poor man* in the *nice suit* as a fool or, alternatively, as the victim of an unscrupulous suit salesman depends on how the teller presents the characters to us. This in turn influences the way we laugh—whether sympathetically or derisively—and hence influences the personalities we reveal in telling and responding to jokes.

Audience Reception of Jokes

Finally, we must consider the reception of the performance of jokes in the conversational context. As Sacks (1974) stresses, the performance of a joke—as opposed to any other sort of narrative—critically depends on laughter for successful completion. The joke acts as the first part of an adjacency pair with laughter as its second part. This open slot following the punch line of a joke offers the listener as coauthor a final opportunity to affect the performance. Certainly audience laughter demonstrates understanding, but at the same time it ratifies and evaluates the teller's performance.

Moreover, since a joke calls for laughter immediately upon its completion, silence on the part of hearers becomes significant. A lack of laughter shows that something has gone awry, but it remains initially ambiguous: Either the recipients have failed to get the joke, that is they failed to pass the understanding test it entails for Sacks and Sherzer, or they are withholding laughter purposely to show that they did not appreciate the performance. If the recipients withhold laughter to comment negatively on the performance, they may have disliked either the actual presentation, say because the teller blew the joke in one of the ways suggested above, or the joke itself, say because it turned out to be one they knew, too childish, too dirty, or what have you.

Beyond simply withholding laughter, members of the audience may respond at the proper juncture with a mirthless *ha-ha-ha,* a disgusted *oh,* or some other sign that they have understood the joke but are not amused. These responses allow the audience to signal that the problem lies not with them, but on the side of the teller. Both initial silence and mirthless laughter often herald some more explicit comment by the audience on the joke performance. We see this in Ned's comments on the first Harvard joke, where he determines that he had heard it before and considered it too dirty to tell in the current conversation.

Listeners may also interrupt the ongoing performance of a joke with appreciative laughter. This laughter does not respond directly to the punch line, and hence cannot count as passing the understanding test the joke poses, on the analyses of Sacks and Sherzer. Instead, it serves as a positive evaluation of the performance, as a sign that the teller is going the extra mile to make the buildup itself entertaining (except in those few instances of jokes scripted with a double punch line, as described by Hockett 1960). Here, too, the laughter may herald evaluation such as Lydia's *Isn't that cute* comment before the final couplet of Brandon's first Harvard joke.

Of course, audiences also comment upon completion of a joke they like, sometimes while they laugh about it and sometimes afterward. We see plenty of comment following all the jokes cited above. In response to the first Red Adair joke, Ned comments *That's pretty cute,* as he finishes laughing, and the teller Brandon says *I liked it.* Then Ned goes on to question the joke's contextual relevance, and Brandon responds to this, as we have seen. Again, following each of the three connected jokes, the recipients comment on various aspects of the performance: for example, Lydia shows her appreciation of the joke itself in saying *It's a funny joke* after laughing at the first Harvard joke; Ned praises the performance of the *nice suit* joke with *I've never heard it done like that;* he also records his familiarity with the text of the first Harvard joke as *it ended up being the same joke I knew.* Finally, Frank comments on the structure of the same joke with *It doesn't end in a preposition.* This recasting of a line from the joke to comment on the joke itself amounts to a very special sort of metajoking, in the sense described in the previous chapter. A discussion of what counts as dirty in jokes begins at the mention of the first Harvard joke, and continues on after it and again after the following joke.

So audiences comment on jokes in all kinds of ways, and some of their comments may lead into talk on serious matters; but not uncommonly, the talk after one joke tends to turn to other jokes. And this happens in one case in the passage cited above following the *nice suit* joke. Thus Sherry asks *Did he tell you his Harvard joke?* as the laughter and comment on Brandon's first joke die down. In doing so, she accomplishes several separate ends at once. First of all, she prevents an impending lull in the talk, and simultaneously counters Lydia's attempt to return to the serious discussion going on before the first joke. At the same time, she steers the conversation in the direction of a joke-telling session by announcing a second joke. But instead of expropriating the floor for a performance of her own, Sherry prefaces a joke and turns the privilege of talking over to her husband, Brandon. This may look like an altruistic turn-passing. And it may be related to gender: Men typically do the joke telling in mixed groups, while women act as the audience. But, after all, it means Sherry is controlling the progress of the interaction in multiple ways, though she will not be talking herself.

A Final Anecdote

By way of contrast, I would like to investigate a final example in which Brandon turns the tables on Sherry and prefaces a performance by her.

LYDIA: I've told the cute story about Elizabeth saying when her mom's ready to go out to the store, "Got the coupons Mom?" I thought that was the cutest thing I'd ever heard.

BRANDON: Did you hear the one the other day? Tell the one about you in the grocery store Sher.

SHERRY: I was- I saw this *new* yogurt. That had only fifty calories. And you know they have the Yoplait that's a hundred and fifty, and the other is ninety, and Weightwatchers has a ninety calorie one- this one was *fif*ty calories and I just looked at it and I went- (1.0) Wow. And Elizabeth said, "What. Did you see a really good price Mom?" Huh huh huh huh [huh huh huh huh.]

LYDIA: [Isn't that em*bar*rassing] ha *ha* ha ha.

SHERRY: Huh heh heh. And I just started *laugh*ing and laughing. And I hugged her. And she was saying, "Well, was it? Was it?" Said "No honey, I"

LYDIA: Maybe you'll have the joy of having *your* children tell *you* . . .

Lydia's story about Elizabeth, a daughter of Sherry and Brandon, naturally suggests a further story to Brandon, which he announces, first with a question directed at the group: *Did you hear the one the other day?,* then with a request directed at Sherry: *Tell the one about you in the grocery store.* This, too, might be seen as gender-related, since Brandon announces and Sherry performs a typically female type of narrative, namely a personal anecdote involving her daughter, rather than the sort of canned jokes men prefer. Sherry's story recounts an experience which builds on the frugal image depicted in Lydia's previous turn.

This personal anecdote clearly does not work as an understanding test in the sense of Sacks and Sherzer, but rather represents a self-revelation narrative of a kind we investigated in chapter 3. Sherry organizes her performance so as to elicit laughter in the middle, rather than at some final punch line. Instead of a punch line as such, the anecdote has a key sentence in which Elizabeth asks a question which reveals Sherry's frugality in a

funny light. And after relating this question, Sherry herself initiates laughter. Lydia joins in after commiserating with *Isn't that
embarrassing?* This provides the perfect response at this point
in the narrative, which then continues. Since the anecdote cen-
ters around an embarrassing moment for Sherry, she must relate
her reaction to what the child asks in order to complete it. The
revelation of personal foibles or embarrassing experiences tends
to elicit minimal laughter, then consolation or a counter-narrative
by another participant revealing similar foibles and embarrassment. And we find exactly this in the passage above, where it
leads to another anecdote, in which Lydia relates an embarrassing
incident from years ago, involving her own children, two of
whom are present as adults now with children of their own.
This response contrasts sharply with the reception we saw
accorded true jokes, where laughter accompanies comments
about how funny the joke was, that it was familiar after all, and
so on.

Conclusions

The presentation and analysis of four jokes and a personal anecdote in this chapter show how a teller and an audience together
negotiate the preface to a joke, the performance itself, and the
reaction to it. Jokes develop cohesively out of serious topical talk
or wordplay; they segue back into serious talk about the content,
quality, or performance of the joke itself—or they suggest further
jokes of similar or different types and on related or unrelated
topics. We have focused on the interactional significance of joke
telling in presenting a self and probing for shared backgrounds
and affiliations, and hence in mutual revelation and consequent
enhancement of rapport. We have seen that effective joke telling
routinely elicits laughter before the actual punch line falls, which
vitiates the analysis of jokes as aggressive tests and correlates
with the view of joking as entertainment. Among adults, the
aggressive testing function of joke telling largely disappears into
a reciprocal process of elicitation, performance, participation,
enjoyment, and evaluation. The teller may even supply crucial
background information to ensure correct understanding and a

successful performance. This fills out the picture of joke telling we began to sketch in chapter 2 from the perspective of external conversational organization, and complements the description of the other humorous narratives from chapter 3.

6

Conclusions and Perspectives

Well, then, that's the humor of't.

Shakespeare, *Henry V,* 2, i, 121 ∎

In this final chapter, I would like to pick up the recurrent themes of this book and spell out their consequences, paying special attention to areas for future work in discourse analysis and humor studies.

Fun Talk

Early on I considered *fun talk* as a title for this book; a friend advised me against it, for two reasons. First, it would give the impression that joking turned a conversation into a special kind of talk, when, as I hope to have shown, joking bubbles up and recedes periodically in the course of almost any conversation. And second, *fun talk* would make conversation laden with joking sound flippant and trivial, when, as I again hope to have shown, joking fulfills many "serious" functions in conversation as well as generating laughter. In fact, the frequency of joking in almost any conversation is less a consequence than a precondition of the research reported here.

At the outset of my work on conversational joking, several people expressed their reservations about its feasibility, because collection of examples would be too difficult. Even then I already had hours and hours of taped conversations filled with humor of all kinds. I found not just the narrative jokes, puns, and sarcasm discussed in the literature on humor, but funny personal anecdotes, complex interactional wordplay, and jointly produced funny narratives as well—overall, more types and instances of humor than earlier research suggests. We are apparently unaware of the amount of joking in our everyday talk. Or we are so accustomed to letting professional writers and comedians entertain us that we feel our own spontaneous efforts at humor cannot measure up. This presumably holds for everyday talk and oral performance generally in the eyes and ears of literate moviegoers and television-viewers.

Nor do we only underrate the quality of our spontaneous humor—even jokes which amused us heartily at the time—we also tend to think of humor as a frivolous accoutrement of talk, perhaps pleasant enough, but certainly unnecessary. In fact, humor has two strikes against it anyway, since it seems to get in the way of the serious business that conversation "ought" to attend to. This bias goes hand in hand with our general cultural conviction that joking and humor are simply not very important. People are baffled to hear that Freud wrote a whole book on jokes; they remain convinced that Shakespeare's tragedies are far superior to his comedies—even those who know nothing of Aristotle's opinion on tragedy versus comedy. Jokes and comedy are morally suspect. So we are blinded to the importance of our conversational joking just as surely as we underestimate its quality. We joke by habit without realizing how our joking works to present a personality, to test for shared attitudes, to identify a common code for our interaction, and generally to keep the conversation moving along so that we can negotiate tasks in a convivial atmosphere.

So one major point of this study is to stress the importance of joking in conversation. Spontaneous joking serves many functions in our everyday talk, often several simultaneously. Previous research on humor routinely mentions its role in smoothing the course of interaction, but no one has ever illustrated any of the relevant processes till now. We have seen how conversationalists use humor especially during greetings and lulls to break the ice and keep the ball rolling, to work through errors and misunderstandings, but also to realign the participants and redefine the interaction or to open a new conversation.

Past research also identified a social control function for joking, which we were able to ascertain in concrete examples. Conversationalists poke fun at ways of speaking, logical blunders, and past experiences generally. One speaker may openly kid another for something just said, or prefer to laugh about the faux pas with a third participant outside the hearing of the first. Our canned jokes target groups or behaviors we want to characterize as ridiculous. The funny anecdotes we relate about ourselves also identify beliefs no longer held and actions we now consider laughable. Both narrative forms thus allow us to distance ourselves from certain people and behavior patterns. We even joke about our own present condition and slips in order to record our embarrassment and elicit sympathy rather than attacks from others.

Moreover, we found that joking often has a metalingual function in conversation—a function overlooked in past work on humor. In particular, joking may target a construction or word choice, and even question incongruities in our regular speaking habits or in the language system itself. Through joking we identify odd patterns and work toward a common way of speaking. Wordplay also makes us attend to relations between phonologically identical or similar words and phrases, so it possesses a metalingual force of its own. Metalingual joking provides participants in talk with data about their own languaging, helps them define the sort of talk appropriate to their interaction, lets them feel they "speak the same language," and hence enhances rapport. At the same time, this joking provides the descriptive linguist with a window on the grammar and meaning emergent in the ongoing conversation.

Overall, joking of all types serves many purposes in conversation. Far from simply providing pleasant icing on the cake, joking inheres in the very substance of talk in interaction and holds it together. And this reflects back on the nature of conversation itself.

The Art of Conversation

Conversationalists store and recycle a wide range of formulaic utterances tailored to specific positions in their everyday talk. We saw stock humorous greetings, topic-changers, leave-takings, and so on. And we found standard joking responses to serious formulaic greetings, leave-takings, and so forth. Then there are the funny personal anecdotes we tell and retell, and the canned jokes we store away and recycle from one conversation to the next. Moreover, we noted that telling one anecdote or joke makes another anecdote or joke topically relevant, so anecdotes and jokes come in series and rounds. The variety and popularity of recycled humorous forms indicates that we expect joking opportunities to recur in much of our conversation—often in similar local contexts.

We saw further that spontaneous joking naturally thrives at the same organizational points where stock forms cluster. Since one sort of humor makes more joking topically appropriate, one pun may turn into competitive wordplay, and a hyperbolic statement may give rise to the interactive construction of an exaggerated description. The frequency and persistence of spontaneous joking in everyday talk suggest that conversation often tends more toward performance and entertainment than to the expeditious exchange of information.

The notion of the customary joking relationship came up repeatedly in our discussions. For some groups or pairs of conversationalists, joking and teasing are the conversational norm. Such speakers may practice joking on a more or less competitive basis, such that one participant sees another as leading or trailing according to some vague scoring procedure. Competitive conversational humorists take advantage of any occasion for mocking, sarcasm, and even apparent insult. Clearly they view conversation as a series of opportunities for joking.

We also investigated the so-called joke-first practice. This strategy for joking taps directly into the call-response structure of the adjacency pair itself, which constitutes the basis for the organization of turn taking in conversation. Thus conversationalists often deliberately misunderstand the first part of an adjacency pair and produce a joke-first in line with the misunderstanding but askew to the appropriate interpretation of the context. This results in punning, teasing, and put-ons. In fact, the mechanism of this joke-first practice is available to any conversationalist who chooses to pretend misinterpretation of the foregoing turn in order to pun on it. The net effect is that any turn at talk presents a potential for wordplay, though, of course, ambiguous phrases lend themselves particularly well.

Taken together, these observations culminate in a view of conversation geared more to fun than work, more like a playground than a place of business. Joking around is a natural part of friendly conversation, because we talk to enjoy ourselves. Even granting that my data overrepresent joking, inasmuch as many of my recordings involve friends and extended family members at leisure enjoying food and drink together, conversation still ends up quite conducive to joking; and research on joking between co-workers from factory personnel to professional colleagues presents a similar picture, especially in certain recurrent environments like greetings, transitions, and taking leave. Any sort of conversation depends on hints and clues that the participants understand each other and agree on what they are doing; joking provides a means of signaling and testing for shared attitudes, so it has a definite role to fill in all kinds of spontaneous interactions.

How Aggressive Is Joking?

Humor has traditionally been associated with aggression in three ways: first, toward some butt—the person or group targeted; second, toward the audience, in submitting them to an understanding test; and third, toward all other participants in the interaction, by disrupting topical turn-by-turn talk and holding the floor to perform for an extended period of time. As to the first type of aggression, recall that we analyzed jokes about a person who pathologically confuses names, a pushy suit salesman, and a supercilious Harvard student; we looked at examples of spontaneous joking which poked fun at the institution of marriage, a movie, the text of a state park leaflet, and so on. The expression of aggression through jokes and joking lets us present a particular personality with our own attitudes and feelings. It lets us probe for similar attitudes and feelings in our listeners. And it may help us let off steam and relieve tension which might find less salubrious expression otherwise.

The second sort of aggression appears in the so-called test function of joking. Joking calls for laughter at a precise point, and hence tests whether the listener can access the crucial background information and process the text in time to laugh appropriately. Since, however, joking ushers in a play frame, even the aggression will not usually have a serious effect. Moreover, precisely because they present little understanding tests, jokes let listeners demonstrate shared knowledge and patterns of thought, which redounds to rapport. Joking exchanges cited in the foregoing chapters as well as those in my recordings as a whole show that the tests imposed by jokes hardly count as real aggression. Witness the joke we analyzed where the teller naturally provided the necessary background information up front to ensure understanding and appreciation. While teenagers may tell jokes, especially dirty jokes, to test others and to show off their own superior knowledge, it seems adults tell jokes to amuse others with their performance and their sense of humor.

Whatever testing or aggression jokes impose, audiences readily acquiesce in them to enjoy the payoff of amusement. Far from attempting to avoid the alleged aggression of jokes, we request others to tell us any good ones they have heard, and we encourage them in their performance. In what also counts as a major conclusion of this study, we observed a high degree of audience participation during presentation of narrative jokes generally, including laughter at appropriate positions before the punch line. Our investigation of concrete joke-telling episodes found performance, participation, and enjoyment primary, while the test function appeared in the form of probing for shared attitudes, and the aggressive tendency otherwise appeared negligible.

Puns are potentially more aggressive than jokes in testing understanding, since they crop up unannounced in the flow of conversation, and allow for listener participation only after the fact. The tests puns impose, like those of jokes, give listeners an opportunity to demonstrate shared background knowledge and logic, which promotes conviviality. This also leads to further joking. Inasmuch as punning introduces a play frame, it naturally spreads to other participants and encourages other forms of wordplay. So although puns disrupt topical talk, they may create a cohesive stretch of conversation in their own right. All in all, puns seem more aggressive than canned jokes, and, of course, some cases of punning will be more aggressive than others. The recognition of varying degrees of aggression between and within types of conversational joking also ranges among the principal conclusions of this investigation.

High on the scale of aggression as compared with jokes and puns are mocking and sarcasm. Mocking someone for a slip of the tongue or making a sarcastic reply to a friendly offer combines the first and second types of aggression: The recipient is both the butt of the joke and the listener taking an understanding test. "Getting" the joke entails admitting a fault or error and laughing at it. So the imposed test goes beyond understanding to composure and a sense of humor about embarrassing matters. Still, this admittedly more threatening aggression is usually mitigated by a customary joking relationship. In such a relationship, kidding counts as positive, friendly politeness by flouting the formal conventions of negative, deferential politeness. Moreover, the reciprocity of the relationship allows the recipient of sarcasm to turn around and mock the sarcastic assailant for a verbal slip or a poorly worded question a moment later. Our consideration of the inherent test function in joking supports the general conclusion that various humorous forms occupy distinct positions along a scale of aggressive force.

The third sort of aggression in joking—interactional aggression in disrupting topical turn-by-turn talk—can appear rather significant in some contexts. We analyzed a long passage in which a single speaker produced three separate narrative jokes in a row. But any joke-teller depends on the goodwill and participation of co-conversationalists in many ways. The series of jokes we investigated grew out of topical talk in a natural way; one listener requested the first Harvard joke and another asked for the second; and each joke elicited ample laughter along with discussion of its content and the whole topic of dirty jokes. The overall effect of the series of jokes is one of an interactional achievement for mutual entertainment rather than of a single speaker monopolizing the floor to the exclusion of others. The passages illustrating wordplay interaction yield the same impression.

Aggression in conversational joking is a matter of degree. Exchanging funny personal anecdotes conduces only to rapport with no aggressive component apparent. Joint production of a funny story again illustrates high rapport and little chance for aggression. Joke telling and punning rank somewhat higher in aggression of the three types identified, though their aggression toward listeners still ends up rather small. Only mocking and sarcasm display a fairly high degree of aggression toward the listener, since they make this listener the butt of the joke as well. Yet even here the force of the play frame, perhaps enhanced by a customary joking relationship, mitigates the actual aggression. Nevertheless, we inspected examples where joking had an apparently negative effect on some interlocutors and resulted in at least cursory apologies. Hence the play frame does not entirely obliterate the threat of an aggressive speech act.

The interplay of the three sorts of aggression within the play frame and the customary joking relationship presents problems for the analysis of any concrete joking exchange. Our differential perceptions of the aggression in joking, its effects on our listeners, its relation to politeness, power, and solidarity make for difficulties in the interpretation of the interaction. We have seen these difficulties reflected in the behavior of the participants themselves, and they loom even larger for our linguistic analysis. Future researchers will find much to ponder in this area.

Future Perspectives

Beyond the complex interrelations between joking and aggression just discussed, the results of this study suggest several avenues for productive future research.

This investigation follows previous studies of humor in assuming a causal connection from joking to laughter, and from shared laughter to enhanced rapport. We have no problem accepting these connections, but no one has ever explained them. It remains unclear to what extent laughter is an innate versus acquired response to certain stimuli, and to what extent it derives from amusement, rather than serving as an interactional signal. Further, why should laughing together create rapport? And how does this sort of rapport compare with that we enjoy in sharing past experiences, troubles, and so on?

Much joking revolves around ambiguity. Conversationalists can take advantage of this ambiguity as a face-saving device. Thus they may resort to joking in invitations, requests, and refusals. At the same time, real humor seems inimical to these speech acts. Many times a facetious tone or a flippant remark can defuse a potential face-threat more effectively than can a genuine joke. I have not delved into these matters here, but they certainly deserve our attention. Data from service encounters, business meetings, and the like seem more likely to shed light on them than the conversations considered here.

I have commented at times on my data base with its concentration on leisure-time interaction between friends and extended family members; I have the impression that other types of talk contain less variety in joking and less joking overall, and some types seem to illustrate more aggressive joking with more of a test function. Service encounters and business transactions between strangers presumably present a rather different picture of humor than socializing among friends. And comparative studies based on different social groups representing various ages, professions, levels of education, races, same versus mixed gender, and so on would certainly reveal other preferences in conversational joking. The classroom, the courtroom, and various work environments would surely yield interesting data on joking interaction as well.

Another natural extension of the present research would be an investigation of the development of joking behavior based on recorded talk in interaction. The complex functions we have observed in adult joking presumably show up one by one in the developmental process, so investigation of interactions between children at various stages might help sort them out. Since children develop joking strategies during the process of acquiring cultural norms regarding politeness and appropriate ways of speaking generally, such investigations could provide interesting perspectives on the interrelation of humor and the sorts of aggression identified here.

We have seen cases where punning disrupts topical turn-by-turn talk. Sometimes talk returns to the foregoing topic more or less directly. The punster may even apologize for interrupting the ongoing interaction as serious talk reestablishes itself. At other times, general banter ensues. Or participants may conspire to create a wordplay exchange built around a single theme. The trajectory the pun initiates depends on how participants perceive their interaction, their relationship, the current topic, and so on. Consequently, close investigation of wordplay in concrete interaction helps us better understand these features of context. Whether or not joking may occur, and if so what types of joking, how far joking may digress from the current topic and for how many consecutive turns before returning to serious topical talk are a measure of how participants see their interaction in terms of solemnity, business versus pleasure, goal-directed versus for its own sake, and so on. Joking serves as a barometer for participants in an interaction, and for the analyst who approaches it from outside as well.

The analysis of conversational joking reflects on the nature of everyday talk, just as insights into talk lead to a fuller understanding of joking exchanges. This interdependence of joking and conversation led me to the research reported on here in the first place; I hope this analysis can spawn increased attention to the interrelation of humor and conversation.

Humor and Conversation

A bibliographical essay

> Punning is an art of harmonious jingling upon words,
> which, passing in at the ears, excites a titillary motion
> in those parts; and this, being conveyed by the animal
> spirits into the muscles of the face, raises the cockles
> of the heart.
>
> Jonathan Swift, "The Art of Punning" ■

Everyday conversation is the natural showplace—or better, playground—of joking; joking everywhere informs the overall progress and the step-by-step construction of conversation. As a matter of course, then, past research on humor has touched on its conversational environment, and research on conversation has touched on the position of joking and laughter. Work on humor has contributed general observations about the role of joking in our talk and particular examples cited from memory.

Linguistically oriented studies of jokes have revealed much about the internal structure of the funny stimulus and, along the way, have also produced inciteful comments on the conversational context of humor. Reseach on natural conversation, by contrast, has focused either on the location of joking and laughter within the talk exchange or on the internal organization of jokes and anecdotes. At the same time, work in linguistic pragmatics, sociolinguistics, and anthropology has sometimes sought to relate such notions as politeness, social distance, group membership, and rapport with conversational joking.

In this appendix, I will attempt to organize the results of these various strands of research insofar as they concern conversational humor. There are many excellent surveys of humor theories, such as Wilson (1979) and McGhee (1979) stressing psychological issues, Apte (1985) from an anthropological perspective, Morreall (1987) from a philosophical point of view, and Raskin (1985) from a linguistic perspective, so I will limit my attention as far as possible to joking in everyday talk in face-to-face interaction— to the wordplay, punning, sarcasm, and telling of funny stories in spontaneous conversation. I would like to consider, first, research on humor as it reflects on talk and interaction, then linguistically oriented research where it touches on joking, and finally the treatment of joking and laughter in conversation analysis.

Humor in Social Interaction

I begin with a more or less chronological review of thought on the role of joking in social interaction. Then I turn to the anthropological literature on so-called "joking relationships," followed by a consideration of psychological research on joking and laughter.

Humor and laughter have attracted the attention of scholars from a wide range of disciplines down through the ages. Since the classical period in Greece, philosophers have concerned themselves with the nature of humor and the causes of laughter. The arguable centrality of the "sense of humor" and laughter as defining attributes of *homo sapiens* or, to beg the question, *homo ridens,* and the omnipresence of joking and laughter in human interaction have enlisted the scholarly interest and effort of psychologists, anthropologists, sociologists, and others.

Sporadic references to the social function of humor appear early on. Plato in the *Philebus* and Aristotle in his *Poetics, Rhetoric,* and *Nicomachean Ethics* see a social value in laughter, since it points out ridiculous behavior to be avoided. Both recognized an element of malice and aggression in joking as well. But Hobbes (1650 and 1651) is most closely associated with the so-called "superiority theory" of humor whereby we laugh because of a feeling of "sudden glory" at the misfortune, errors, and defects of others. In his critical response to Hobbes, Hutcheson (1750) points out the contagious nature of laughter and its importance in the creation of friendship. He argues that laughter at faults provides a better "social corrective" than does serious admonition. Joking enlivens our conversation and occasions pleasure for joker and audience.

Bergson (1899) was the first writer to give significant attention to the interactional aspects of humor and laughter. He points out the difficulty we have in appreciating the comic in isolation from other people. Laughter, he felt, always implies a real or imagined complicity with other laughers. Participants in a group conspire to laugh at one of their number for some mechanical foible or slip, some inflexible attitude or habit of mind. So laughter has a social function of identifying inappropriate behavior. The aggressive laughter of others and our consequent embarrassment lead us to modify our behavior to better match that of the group and to react more flexibly to situations.

Sully (1902) discusses the social corrective function of laughter, though he stresses its role in the creation of gaity and, hence, more pleasurable participation in social life. Laughter is contagious; it has a "choral" function which nurtures group solidarity. Laughter at outsiders further enhances cohesion within the group, but it also affects members of the group laughed at: They may either alter their laughable behavior or adhere to it all the more tenaciously. In addition, Sully related laughter to play. Enjoyment of a funny event derives from sudden arousal of a "play mood"—a refusal to take the event seriously, which is a central feature of play.

Freud (1905) touches on a number of themes central to the analysis of joking in conversation. First of all, he suggests that joking serves as a substitute for aggression, sexual or otherwise. Joking lets us enjoy our repressed feelings in a masked, socially acceptable way. This presupposes a three-party interaction with a joke-teller, a listener, and the butt of the joke, the victim of its aggression. The teller demonstrates cleverness and displays a self or personality; but the listener does so as well: Only what the listener allows to be a joke *is* a joke—otherwise it is just a, perhaps humorous, story (105). Laughter at the crucial juncture signals understanding of a joke as a joke. Freud made much of the difference between the true joke and the humorous story, between wit and humor generally, which we can disregard here;

central to our concern in the following is Freud's recognition of
the interactional and interpersonal dynamic of joking. For a joke
to be successful, the teller and listener must share inhibitions
with regard to the sort of aggression and feelings expressed.
Laughing at the same jokes is evidence of far-reaching psychical
conformity. Here again we see the rapport function of joking,
though Freud—as in so many other areas—describes a far more
elaborate background for this function than do his predecessors.

Eastman (1936) argues that "fun" forms the basis of humor,
and he explicitly identifies "being in fun" as the natural state of
the child at play. Adults require special conditions and jokes to
get themselves back into this childlike state of fun. Eastman sees
frustrated expectations and offenses as the essence of all jokes.
But joking and mocking make "fun" of aggression and criticism;
they stress the play rather than the person at whose expense we
laugh, so they end up much less hurtful than a serious reprimand
or other corrective action.

In a series of articles, Bateson (1953; 1954; 1956; 1969) concluded that the way we "frame" our actions—either as serious
or play—determines the reactions they elicit just as much as do
the actions themselves. Any action carries its own message of
aggression, disinterest, or what have you along with a "metamessage" which frames it as serious or play. We frame our actions
and talk through various sets of signals and hints (like the "con-
textualization cues" of Gumperz 1982a, 1982b): We may deliver
any utterance with the metamessage "This is play"; and once
we have established a "play frame," anything we say can elicit
laughter, even otherwise aggressive talk. The explosive moment
in humor comes when the relation between the implicit
"ground" and the focused "figure" dissolves and reverses, so
that the metamessage turns into the message. This brings to
conscious attention previously backgrounded elements; since
this background will often involve the pain of others, it will seem
as if we laugh at this pain, though in fact this is just an associated
emotion, not the cause of humor.

Both Goffman and Fry have built on Bateson's notion of the
play frame in ways that reflect on joking in interaction, Goffman
applying the notion to a broad spectrum of interactional phenomena, and Fry concentrating on humor as such.

Goffman (1955) notes the use of a joking manner to aid in the negotiation of face-threatening acts, and the use of wisecracks and repartee to "make points" in aggressive "face work." He also investigates many facets of play, touching on joking at several junctures (1961). He finds both a stress-reduction function and a social control function in joking. In recurrent groupings, the right to make a joke of something may belong only to the ranking person present. According to Goffman, some cases of laughter exemplify the "flooding out" of emotions when an individual momentarily loses the ability to maintain a serious frame due to the tension inherent in it. Flooding out in laughter is contagious, so other participants may join the first in breaking the frame, but they may also cling to the frame and ignore the laughter. And, of course, we sometimes tease someone just to see if we can get them to flood out. Goffman (1974) relates framing to the notion of "key" first introduced by Hymes (1972; see below): A humorous key involves a systematic transformation of a situation, which determines what we perceive as going on in it, for instance kidding Al as opposed to insulting him. This transformation may require complicity on the part of the victim, playing along with the kidding, perhaps even putting on a show of anger or embarrassment at the disclosure of the jest. Cues and "bracketing" in time and space ensure that participants recognize frames and see that others do so as well. Goffman considers unseriousness and kidding so standard in everyday talk that we need special statements to exclude them, for instance *Now I'm really serious about this.* He treats kidding among other "benign fabrications" like leg-pulls, practical jokes, surprise parties, and so on.

Fry (1963) extended the notion of the play frame to the analysis of joke telling and other forms of humor. He distinguishes "canned" jokes, which we generally recall from past conversations and recycle rather than invent, from "spontaneous" joking, which arises within the ongoing interaction and cannot usually weather the transition to another context successfully. We typically announce the telling of a canned joke with formulaic phrases like *I've got a joke for you;* the teller may even laugh a little during the buildup to show amusement, though too much premature laughter tends to spoil the joke for the listeners. This introduces the play frame necessary for enjoyment of humor. Fry stresses the importance of the punch line to the joke proper. The unexpected punch line causes sudden laughter, and distinguishes the joke from other activities such as games and dreams which also take place in an ongoing play frame.

In a similar vein, Lorenz (1963) suggests that laughter derives from aggressive behavior phylogenetically, and retains some of its primitive motivation. In particular, laughter evolved through ritualization of a threatening movement; it forms an immediate bond among participants, but it also draws a line against outsiders: first those who cannot laugh along, and second those at whom the laughter aims. Lorenz stresses the role of humor both as a social corrective and as a form of self-perception. We laugh at our own excesses and foibles just as we laugh at those of others.

Based on his extensive study of dirty jokes, Legman (1968) sees joke telling as direct aggression: The teller seeks to slough off anxiety about the joke's subject matter by exposing the listener to the same anxiety. In doing so, the teller can achieve a kind of superiority by being the only one who does not laugh. The listener's laughter signals a complicity in the aggression of the joke, which "shrives" the teller, and in turn places the listener under a compulsion to become the next teller. Legman overstates the hostility of joke telling, because he does not take into account its character as a ritualization of aggression à la Lorenz, and because he misses the metamessage which accompanies the joke to establish a play frame à la Bateson. Although he mentions all-night joking sessions, he seems to deny the sociability of joking; and despite the intricate interaction between the teller and the listener, he overlooks the rapport function of humor. Nevertheless, the central insight remains that a joke tests the listener's understanding of and attitude toward its subject matter.

Wilson (1979) identifies both personal and social functions of joking. Among the personal functions, he discusses joking to reduce hostility and to foster rapport, to express rebelliousness, to broach sensitive topics in an ambiguous way, thus giving the listener the option of responding seriously or with laughter. The social functions of joking are oriented toward preserving the status quo. They include easing friction, reducing anxiety, expressing ridicule without repercussions, especially as a safety valve to release aggressions of minorities and out-of-power groups generally. But Wilson also mentions the social control function of humor in labeling deviant behavior as laughable, and thus in enforcing conformity through fear of being laughed at. In this regard, he noted that public joking flows down the social pyramid with superiors laughing at inferiors, in-groups at out-groups, and normal groups at fringe groups.

Back in 1960, Coser had reported on her observation of staff meetings in a psychiatric hospital, noting that humor was routinely directed downwards in the hierarchy. Senior staff members joked about junior members, while junior members joked about themselves, their patients, and their families. Thus their humor tended toward self-disparagement. Any humor directed at superiors was—understandably—exchanged only in private outside the hearing of superiors.

According to Fine (1983), joking has both control functions and conflict functions. Laughing, kidding, and satire reveal expectations and enforce norms within the group, whereas sarcasm, irony, and parody direct aggression at outsiders. Humor tempers our aggression against outsiders, but still serves to unify the group, since laughter communicates approval to the joker and shared laughter signals shared perspectives. Within the group, humor fulfills three requirements: It must be comprehensible, inoffensive, and functional, in that it supports group control or relief of tension.

Pollio (1983) suggests that humor frees us from external constraints such as social forces and group pressure, rather than from internal inhibitions (as Freud argued). Consequently, we feel freer to laugh among friends than among strangers or superiors, since we need not hide our emotions from friends. Since humor allows us to step outside the normal bounds of politeness and order, it gains momentary freedom from these social constraints for us. Within the group, joking is not really aggressive at all. In fact, the frequent target of joking may well enjoy high status in the group; being attacked gives those targeted a chance to show they "can take it." Laughing and joking reach out to others, show attention to them, and move toward greater involvement with them.

Chapman (1983) recognizes many simultaneous functions and

effects of humor on the joker, the target, and the audience: It may simultaneously increase hostility against outsiders and solidify good feelings within the group. Chapman reviews research showing the importance of preparation, situation, and companions for appreciation of humor, amount and type of laughter. Even nonhumorous laughter, as in tickling, depends greatly on immediate surroundings and company present. Especially laughter by others present facilitates our laughing as a response to humor. Preferences for certain kinds of humor also vary with companions and surrounding, for example mixed sex versus same sex groups. Chapman finds that humor helps promote intimacy at the same time it supplies relief from discomfort caused by intimacy increasing too rapidly; it helps us pry for information, issue a rebuke, and disclose attitudes.

Ziv (1984) returns to the social control function of humor as well as its rapport function. Humor enforces the social order, since we laugh at outsiders and as a punishment for violation of norms. It contributes to the structure and hierarchy of society: Higher-status individuals joke openly about lower-status ones, while the latter direct jokes at their social superiors only in private, where humor may serve to release tension. But Ziv also stresses the role of humor as a key to opening and enhancing interpersonal relations, in testing for shared knowledge and narrowing social distance. Inside jokes develop group identity and uniqueness, so that "humor also creates a common language" (33).

Schutz (1989) argues for ethnic jokes in particular that they have different functions within the group and across groups. Ethnic humor expresses aggression, but in a form muted by its impersonality and general stereotypes. Jokes about national stereotypes or ethnic groups in a particular society facilitate interaction and assimilation in nonaggressive ways. They show all the control functions we have seen for the society at large, and they can also serve cohesive and rapport functions both within the target group and for other groups as well.

Beginning with Sully's relation of laughter to play, then especially since Bateson introduced the notion of the play frame, writers on humor have shown an increasing tendency to downplay the aggression in joking—with the exception of Legman, whose focus on very dirty jokes explains his emphasis on the aggressive element. Pollio denies joking any aggressive moment at all within the group. But we have certainly all felt hurt or angry about some joking remark a friend made in the spirit of play. And we all recall situations where a parent, teacher, or boss playfully exchanged personal jokes until some threshold was reached, then abruptly became serious and warned *That goes a little too far* or simply took advantage of a higher authority to end the interaction. Apparently, then, the play frame neither completely dissolves power relationships nor obliterates the message our talk would have if taken seriously. This coincides with Lorenz's hypothesis that laughter developed from, and in some degree still reflects, an aggressive movement.

In fact, Bateson initially formulated his ideas of the play frame based on observation of animals at play. He explicitly notes that the playful act continues to denote the corresponding serious act and may turn back into hostility if a proper balance is not maintained. The dog growling and baring its teeth still threatens, but the wagging tail hints that we need not take the threat seriously; still, two dogs may have to spar for some time before it becomes clear whether they are fighting or playing. In play, as in ritual, one act stands for another act, but does not count as that second act *really;* nevertheless, even among friends with a history of joking, a playful jab may hit a raw nerve. And the consequences may include serious emotional outbreaks or talk as well as humorous responses. Seeming aggression can be funny if taken in the spirit of play, but the play frame does not entirely obliterate the aggressive moment, which may reemerge with various possible consequences.

This interrelation of joking and aggression reappears in different guises in all kinds of humor research, as does the notion of the play frame. What we have called the social control function of humor—the idea that laughter enforces norms—and its "rapport function" of narrowing social distance, revealing shared attitudes, and enhancing group cohesion also figure prominently in past studies of humor. Finally, the interactional dynamic of joking is central. The successful performance of a canned joke depends on the listener as well as on the teller: We must announce our jokes and establish a play frame, perhaps with a little laughter, but not too much; at the same time, the listener must accept the play frame and take the joke as a joke, along with having the necessary background knowledge to get the joke and laugh at the proper juncture. Unannounced spontaneous joking requires even closer attention to context and good timing to succeed.

Joking Relationships

Radcliff-Brown (1940) described "joking relationships" institutionalized in certain tribal societies on the basis of clan, descent, or marriage. Ethnographers have identified many such kin-based joking relationships in the tribal societies of Africa, Asia, North America, and Oceania. The partners in such relationships participate by custom in certain patterned types of joking, teasing, insult, and horseplay, perhaps along with other social obligations. The joking relationship may be reciprocal or nonreciprocal, with both partners or only one doing the joking, but in either case, it requires that the recipient of joking may not take offense. Such relationships may hold between preferred marriage partners, and, in these cases, they often serve to promote familiarity and sexual involvement, but the joking tends to support cultural norms by attacking disapproved sexual behavior. In general, joking relationships help maintain social order, release aggressions in a public, acceptable way, and foster solidarity.

Douglas (1968) stresses the importance of the total social situation in the determination of what counts as a joke. Though much of the behavior in joking relationships seems like gross insult and obscenity, it becomes humorous by revealing incongruities in the relationship. A joke cannot be perceived as a joke unless it corresponds to our social experience. While joking appears to challenge established patterns in society, it represents only a "temporary suspension of the social structure," which depends upon consensus for recognition. So joking ultimately clarifies and enforces social norms.

As anthropologists continued to study joking relationships, they began to find similar pairings between members of the same age-group, in different villages, and in different occupational groups.

This went hand in hand with increased interest in the non-kin joking relationships in industrial societies. These joking relationships are formed voluntarily by individuals in frequent contact, often within a work setting.

Thus Sykes (1966) observed workers in a Glasgow factory and discovered that all kinds of sexual banter and horseplay took place in public, for example between old men and young women, but not between young men and women. He hypothesized that gross obscenities were only exchanged between workers who were not potential sexual partners, which amounts to a reversal of tribal kin-based patterns.

In the same vein, Pilcher (1972) described joking among longshoremen in Portland, Oregon, and found a clear separation for them between the work domain and the private and family one. Broad vulgarity, dirty jokes, nicknames, and swearing are confined to working hours with no spillover into private or family life. The longshoremen severely sanctioned the use of nicknames and crude joking outside the work domain.

Based on his research at a factory in northern England, Linstead (1988) conceptualized humor as a framework for "play" activity in the industrial setting. He recognizes an "exploration" function for joking in allowing a message to be risked; a "boundary" function in defining appropriate behavior by ridiculing out-group propensities; a "coping" function in defusing aggression and distancing unpleasant facts. He argues that canned jokes do not differ so much from situation humor as often claimed: He found canned jokes were retold, reformulated, and incorporated into the context, which, in turn, helped determine their significance.

According to Goody (1978), joking relationships are interactions characterized by a prior premise of nonthreatening intention, no matter how sexual or aggressive the behavior appears. She stresses the particular histories of joking partners, both as individuals and in their common past encounters. For participants in a joking relationship, the sheer weight of their previous experience with each other makes it impossible for them to really take offense, quarrel, or make love. So the joking relationship provides a serviceable tool for enabling continued interaction between people who must depend upon each other. It is the structure of the relationship itself that determines the intention participants attribute to the acts they perform. And this holds for institutionalized kin-based joking relationships as well as for voluntary non-kin ones.

Wilson (1979) summarizes work on tribal kin-based joking relationships and their counterparts in industrial society. He tends to focus on their sexual significance, and sees a consistency across cultures in the use of joking to express sexual attraction, though the joking in industrial societies reflects personal choice rather than tribal organization.

Apte (1985) provides an in-depth, critical treatment of both kin and non-kin joking relationships. He points to the fundamental dichotomy between the two: Kin-based joking relationships in tribal society are obligatory, normative, and either reciprocal or nonreciprocal, whereas non-kin relationships in industrial society are voluntary, generally reciprocal partnerships between friends. Apte (1983) pointed out the function of non-kin joking relationships in "controlling"real aggression and "stabilizing" the group by releasing this aggression in a nonviolent way. Customary joking relationships between professional or other social groups demonstrate group identity and foster solidarity.

The idea that people in close social contact sometimes develop a customary joking relationship plays a key role in the discussion above to account for the rapport function of apparently impolite or aggressive behavior. As in Bateson's play frame, which metacommunicates nonserious intent for seemingly hostile behavior, a past history of enjoyable joking encounters allows friends and colleagues to express apparent insults and impudences not just with impunity, but with comic effect. Of course, participants must avoid truly harmful behavior and continue to signal their playful intentions in order to keep the relationship on keel, but reciprocal "dishing it out" with a smile and "taking it" with laughter generally suffice for this purpose.

Psychological Aspects of Laughter and Humor

Freud (1905) theorized that jokes allow a release for repressed feelings in a socially acceptable way. Obscene jokes express a degree of exhibitionism, just as aggressive jokes express sadism.

Hence we present a particular personality through joking whether we want to or not. The joke-teller and the audience for a joke must share inhibitions and repress the same crucial emotions for the joke to excite laughter.

By contrast, Mindess (1971) sees humor as liberation from external constraints which society imposes on us. We can express our hostility in humor, and thus liberate ourselves from conformity, morality, reason, redundancy, egotism, and so on. At the same time, our joking liberates our listeners as well, so it creates a bond. Of course we also joke to amuse each other, to gain recognition and applause, particularly since a good sense of humor is among the most important personality traits regularly identified.

Goodchilds (1972) tested reactions to wit and sarcasm in small groups with questionnaires, where wit was operationalized as total laughs elicited during group interaction. She determined that being witty increased a participant's scores for "influence" and "popularity." The successful funny wit was most chosen as popular, while the unfunny sarcastic wit was never chosen. Men joked more than women, and only men joked sarcastically. The wit was judged helpful and creative, though the sarcastic wit was judged most influential, and the funny wit was judged most likable.

Based on a summary of relevant sociological work on humor, Martineau (1972) argues that joking has both cohesive and disruptive effects in the group. Traditional joking relationships resolve hostility in structural relations between groups by introducing conflict in an acceptable form. But humor also controls the group in expressing what cannot be expressed otherwise. It can either esteem or disparage those within or outside the group. Within the group, humor may foster hostility toward outsiders and promote cohesion, but it may also introduce conflict and make a bid to change the basis of interaction.

Kane, Suls, and Tedeschi (1977) agree with Martineau, but ask why we use humor to these ends when literal praise and criticism could accomplish the same goals. They stress the ambiguity of joking, which allows for "social recovery" in case of an unfavorable response. Humor provides a safe way to approach taboos and ingratiate powerful others; to probe values and motives; to initiate intimacy; to save face in embarrassing moments. Furthermore, laughter initiates a cognitive transformation of a serious situation into a nonserious one.

The routine equation of humor and laughter comes under scrutiny in La Fave, Haddad, and Maesen (1976). They argue that humor is neither a sufficient nor a necessary condition for laughter, and laughing is not a sure sign of amusement, for example in tickling and nervous laughter. They further claim there is no such thing as a sense of humor, if it means 'the ability to laugh at yourself', since, at best, one facet of my present self laughs at another facet or at an earlier self. Moreover, they maintain, "there are no jokes" (84), but only texts dependent on the audience, context, and culture for understanding and appreciation. La Fave, Haddad, and Maesen recognize the social control function of humor in saying incongruity is especially funny when it results from accidental nonconformity to a social norm. La Fave (1977) reiterates his contention that there are no jokes. And he notes that an extreme insult is funnier than a mild insult, presumably because it more clearly signals playful intention.

La France (1983), too, questions the equation of laughter and mirth. Laughter not only fails as a sure sign of mirth, but more laughter does not necessarily signify greater mirth. Laughter, like other expressive behaviors, can be both "indicative" and "communicative," that is it may reveal mirth at the same time it signals understanding. But precisely because listeners may signal understanding by laughing, we can at least view laughter as a sign of the perception of humor, the recognition of a joke.

Suls (1983) presents a nice review of incongruity theories of humor and psychological research based on them. He recognizes three necessary elements in the humorous event: a play cue, some incongruity, and correct timing. Timing is crucial in both the buildup and the resolution of a joke. The buildup must be neither too short to create arousal, nor too long to hold attention; the punch line must not require too much processing time for resolution. Suls also discusses "metahumor," joking which plays off standard joke structure, as when professional comedians get laughs by commenting on their own jokes or delivery.

From the psychological perspective, we see that joking and laughter have consequences for social interaction as well as for the individual. Joking can introduce conflict into a group, just as it can promote cohesion and rapport. Especially since wit makes a group participant more likable and influential, we can use humor to steer the course of group interaction. At the same time, the ambiguity of humor makes it a serviceable device for testing the social climate and expressing potentially sensitive topics. Psychologists have repeatedly stressed the dependency of humor on the particular context and the tenuous connection between the funny event, amusement, and laughter.

Linguistic Approaches to Humor In Interaction

Literature in the areas of structural linguistics, sociolinguistics, and linguistic pragmatics has sometimes touched on interactional aspects of joking, but the comments tend to be brief and the analyses only suggestive, since the principal focus of this work usually lies elsewhere. I would like to review briefly a fairly mixed bag of such sources with an eye to their thematic relation as well as their chronological order. I begin with Hymes who, as the foremost representative of the "Ethnography of Speaking," is centrally concerned with language in interaction, then report on an ethnographic contribution by Philips; the roughly chronological order of the remaining sources reflects their increasing attention to talk in naturally occurring interaction.

Hymes comments briefly but insightfully on joking in interaction at several points in his work. In 1972 and 1974, he identifies *joke* as an example of a speech act within a larger speech event such as a conversation. He goes on to note that we may deliver any given utterance in some "key" or other, for instance in a "mocking" key by contrast with a "serious" key. The mocking key seems to correspond roughly to Bateson's metamessage "This is play," while the hints and clues which go into establishing a mocking, serious, perfunctory, or painstaking key would correspond to the framing of an interaction generally; see Goffman (1974) for a detailed discussion of these relations.

Philips (1975) offers an interesting description of punning to tease and put people on. Her data derive from field work among Plains and Plateau Indians of the northwest United States; she writes down her examples from memory and notes laughter only sporadically, since she focuses on the cultural/interactional significance of these events rather than on their humor as such. Philips recognizes various classes of puns, including nonverbal examples such as chopping a deck of cards in half in response to "Cut the cards." Puns often arise in this way from a deliberate misunderstanding of some phrase close or identical in form to some other phrase with contrasting meaning. Of course, we may pretend misunderstanding of an ambiguity without actually producing a pun in response to it. But either way, we put someone on in pretending the misunderstanding is real, and we tease both the person deluded and any observers who go along with the pretense. The instigator may laugh or smile during the punning response to signal the put-on and teasing. Finally, Philips stresses the importance of an interactional approach to teasing and put-ons, attending to the efforts of the victim and any others playing along.

Hockett (1960) provides a glowing exception to my claim that linguists have not busied themselves with the topic of humor. His extended structural analysis of joke types grew out of his earlier work on slips of the tongue. Though Hockett's main thrust was taxonomic, he makes several interesting points about joking in interaction. For one thing, he reiterates the importance of context for the appreciation of humor: A sense of propriety for others and a feeling for what we consider sacred limit the range of tellable and laughable jokes in any given situation. In a related vein, joking may serve to sort out and classify participants in a group as to their distinct attitudes. Hockett also points to joking forms smaller than the joke itself, such as the "free-floating" punch and the "latent wisecrack" which we weave into conversation in special contexts, for instance *If you want to get ahead, don't tilt the glass* to someone pouring beer. As to the actual performance of the narrative joke, Hockett hypothesizes that we memorize only the punch line and maybe a few key parts verbatim; the body of the joke we recall only in a nonverbal skeleton form which we flesh out during telling.

Although Grice began by doing Philosophy of Language, his work has become such a staple of linguistic pragmatics that I cannot avoid placing it here in this review. Grice (1967, 1978) portrays irony as a violation of his so-called "conversational maxims." The maxims represent rules for logical, expeditious talk which speakers act as if they were following. They consist in rules like be brief, be orderly, be relevant, an so on. Apparent violations lead listeners to search for an interpretation in line with the overarching "Cooperative Principle" as follows: If you say *Nice tie* but I know you do not like paisley ties, I will construct an interpretation for your utterance assuming you intended something special in violating the maxim of quality (dictating that we should tell the truth), namely, that you want me to recognize that you are following a convention whereby one says the opposite of what one intends. So I infer that you were speaking ironically and do not in fact like the tie at all, especially since irony always reflects a hostile or derogatory judgment. Grice sees irony as pretending and expecting the pretense to be recognized, but he says nothing of the relation of irony or pretending to humor.

Another philosopher, Morreall (1983) shows how we can create humor by violating any one of Grice's maxims or submaxims as well as conventions of politeness, taboos, and so on. Morreall argues that humor facilitates interaction, for instance in breaking the ice, smoothing over errors and bad feelings, softening potentially confrontational requests or topics, because it gives us distance from the practical aspects of the situation and promotes rapport. For the same reasons, humor may be exploited for persuasion and manipulation. Morreall also points to a category of metahumor in comments about the quality of a joke or its relative effectiveness in eliciting laughter from an audience.

Lakoff scatters notes on joking through her work on politeness, power, and gender in conversation. Lakoff (1973) mentions joking, irony, and exaggeration as ploys normal in informal conversation. In a further discussion (1977), she writes that irony inheres in the nature of the situation itself: It may include the speaker, since it need not be directed at anyone in particular, whereas sarcasm always involves an attack. Both irony and sarcasm turn on the representation of a proposition by its opposite, but no direct substitution of the contrary suffices for sarcasm since it always implies aggression against someone. Lakoff (1982) calls humor in ordinary conversation a permissible violation of

Grice's maxim of manner, a conventional sort of circumlocution; Lakoff identifies flippancy and joking by a political leader as violations of the maxim of quality (1990), as Grice indicates for irony. Still, in both cases, joking around builds camaraderie.

According to Cutler (1974), irony always involves approbation on its literal reading, either (1) because the speaker is quoting an opinion expressed by someone else present (Cutler's "provoked irony") or (2) because the speaker simply expresses the opposite of what is meant without allusion to other opinions expressed ("spontaneous irony"). Cutler thus distinguishes provoked cases like *So Sue will win, huh?* (which someone claimed) from spontaneous ones like *Nice tie* (which no one would maintain of such a tie).

Kaufer (1981) defines irony so broadly as to include litotes and other forms of counterstatement. But then it simply conveys an "evaluation" different from the one expressed rather than its propositional negation or opposite. Kaufer further notes the conventionality of certain ironic statements such as *A likely story* which seem impossible to use without irony.

First Sperber and Wilson (1981) and then Sperber (1984) formulate an account of irony which contrasts with those presented so far; see Clark and Gerrig (1984) for critical comment. Sperber and Wilson distinguish irony from parody. In parody we repeat the actual form of our victim's talk or performance, and so are pretending. In irony, by contrast, we reproduce the content of the victim's talk or thought in our own words, and are therefore not pretending: We "mention" as opposed to "use" the meaning or proposition of another. So Sperber and Wilson reject Grice's "pretense" theory and his simple account whereby the intended meaning replaces the stated meaning. They bring Cutler's two separate types of irony into a single account, since a speaker may mention something actually said previously or an opinion tacitly conveyed, say by someone wearing a particular tie. The distinction between pretending or role-play and parody, on the one hand, versus mentioning and irony, on the other hand, comes in for discussion in my analyses of some conversational joking episodes in the body of the text.

Brown and Levinson (1978) invoke joking at several points in their development of a universal account of politeness. They identify joking as a strategy for claiming common ground based on shared membership in a group. But most of the examples they cite would hardly elicit laughter; instead, they signal light-heartedness, nonseriousness, a lack of importance or urgency. Joking works as the so-called "positive" politeness of friendship we use to show solidarity, as opposed to the "negative" politeness of distance we employ to show deference. Joking tends to minimize distance and reduce the threat of requests and impositions. Brown and Levinson also remark on the use of joking insults to assert intimacy, noting that conventionalized or ritualized insults can serve as a mechanism for stressing solidarity because they flout the usual constraints of negative politeness. This recalls the literature on joking relationships reviewed above.

Lehrer (1983) taped and analyzed conversations between small groups asked to taste and classify wines. She found frequent attempts at humor, and saw multilayered effects for them. Thus while humor interrupts the conversation as an information exchange, it furthers the interaction in terms of bonding, at the same time providing momentary relief from the pressure of the task at hand. Participants also used humor to avoid making or defending serious claims about the wines. On the whole, of course, humor contributed greatly to the general enjoyment of the interactions.

Tannen (1984) presents an analysis of the spontaneous talk among a group of friends at a Thanksgiving dinner with a chapter on irony and joking which represents the first extended treatment of humor in natural conversation. Her theoretical concern with differences in conversational styles leads to a focus on variation in the performance and appreciation of humor. She found that joking correlated with more voluable, high-involvement speaking styles generally, and made a person's presence in the conversation more strongly felt. Beyond parody and funny stories, participants used close repetition of the previous utterance with a clever twist for comic effect; they jointly produced jokes and other humorous exchanges. Based on her notion of the paradoxical interrelation of power and solidarity, Tannen (1986, 1989, 1990) has shown how telling jokes can work as a strategy for enhancing intimacy, but also for controlling the conversation; joking redounds to mutual revelation when everyone gets a turn, but it can become a competitive strategy for gaining status as well. In line with our discussion of customary joking relationships above, Tannen (1990) notes that the ritual combat of competitive verbal dueling and reciprocal teasing can also serve to enhance rapport.

My own work on interactional aspects of joking begins with preformed humorous forms such as quips, exaggerated comparisons, and witty repartees which we intersperse in our casual talk (Norrick 1984). Since many stock witticisms flout politeness conventions and taboos, they tend to occur in interaction among friends, where they signal mutual rejection of formal conventions rather than aggression, and thus enhance rapport. In 1986, I investigated the relation between frames (schemas/scripts) and the various genres of recycled verbal humor from stock quips to narrative jokes. In 1989, I began to develop a perspective on conversational humor which takes into account the interactional achievement of the joking performance by a teller and audience and the mutual revelation of self they accomplish in the process. I continued to elaborate this interactional perspective on joking (Norrick 1993a; 1993b), and began to explore the metalingual aspect of conversational humor.

So linguistically oriented research offers useful perspectives on the forms of canned and spontaneous humor, as well as the joking performance and its position and role in conversation; it has illuminated the relations between such notions as parody, irony, pretending, and inference; between punning, deliberate misunderstanding, teasing, and put-ons; and between politeness, power, solidarity, and joking, which reflects on the customary joking relationship. The notion of the mocking *key* extends our understanding of framing and play in the speech event.

Conversation Analysis

Growing out of the pioneering work of Harvey Sacks, Conversation Analysis espouses the microanalysis of everyday talk in interaction as a sociological method, but its influence on linguists engaged in discourse analysis has been enormous. Particularly Gail Jefferson has concerned herself with the meticulous transcription of everyday talk, including laughter, which provides most of the conventions I use in representing conversations in the body of this volume, so I will begin with her work.

Jefferson (1972) points out that questioning repeats often pick out an error in the foregoing utterance and count as a challenge to the original speaker, especially when they contain laughter. She further notes that a laughing repeat serves to signal termination of talk with reference to the item repeated. Jefferson (1979) shows how speakers may use laughter at the end of their utterances to invite listeners to laugh; recipients typically join in just after the onset of laughter, to show appreciation, though they may decline to laugh by pursuing serious talk during the first speaker's laughter. Recipient silence may elicit further attempts to invite laughter, and the first speaker may even prompt listeners with an explicit statement like *That was a joke*. Jefferson (1984a; 1984b) investigates the use of laughter to reduce tension in talk about troubles and to transition into a new topic. Speakers may legitimately laugh in reporting troubles to exhibit that they are "troubles-resistive," but the recipient typically does not join in this sort of laughter, preferring to remain receptive to the serious aspect of the troubles; still, the troubles-teller may bring the recipient to laugh over a series of moves in which the teller indicates a "time-out" from the main topic.

Jefferson (1985) explores several issues surrounding the transcription of laughter, and demonstrates the importance of the placement of laughter for an understanding of the organization of conversation. Laughing may be a matter of flooding out in the sense of Goffman (1961), where the speaker simply cannot contain the laughter and lets it invade the talk being produced, and laughter may also be managed as an interactional resource. In both cases, however, laughter may affect only one or two crucial words, and careful transcription is necessary to show exactly where it occurs and how it distorts speech. Jefferson, Sacks, and Schegloff (1976) point out how a joking move with laughter by one speaker which elicits laughter from a listener can segue into further joking and laughter with reference to the initial joke, as in the example below.

NED: I check the oil about every say fifteen or twe-(hehe)nty (h)*min*utes.

BRANDON: Huh huh huh huh huh huh huh.
     NED::   Huh heh heh heh. Huh huh huh huh. Huh (h)I just
              che(he)ck-
BRANDON: Every day.
     NED: Huh ha ha ha ha ha ha ha.

Finally, they show how laughing together can be managed as a resource for the solution of various interactional problems, particularly in negotiating agreement following offensive talk by one participant.

Schenkein (1972) investigates the use of *hehheh* in conversation to signal nonserious intent in one's own utterance and to demonstrate understanding of nonserious intent in a foregoing utterance by someone else. A *hehheh* from a second speaker can thus be heard as supporting the nonseriousness of the first, and thereby reveals a coincidence of attitude, sense of humor, and the like. Consequently, withholding a *hehheh* from an appropriate slot shows a lack of interest and agreement,while a *hehheh* which draws attention to itself in an inappropriate slot can point out an error or foolishness on the part of the original speaker.

Sacks provided the first investigation of puns in natural conversation and the first careful examination of the course of a joke's telling in conversation. For Sacks (1973:139) a pun consists in the "presence of a word, phrase or other construction of more than one meaning, one meaning being used in the understanding of the construction in the conversational locus, while the other meaning(s) are also fitted to the locus, although in different ways." A pun may occur within the scope of a single turn, may be unintentional, and need not elicit laughter or any other sign of recognition; in fact, only one of Sacks's examples seems to cause amusement, and this may be either nervous laughter or laughter to signal transition to a new topic. Sacks shows that utterances which pun on some aspect of a foregoing story or other segment of conversation are especially adapted to the response slot immediately following that segment, where they serve to demonstrate understanding. In particular, a pun within a proverbial phrase or cliché at a story completion point to show understanding of the story "locates" the word or phrase punned on within that story. And in general, whatever foregoing materials we must identify to understand the punning remark will contain the elements punned on as well.

Sacks (1974) showed that the performance of a joke follows the pattern for story telling generally; the major difference consists in the expected response of laughter for the joke. He illustrates the finely tuned organization of the teller's performance with the response of the audience at a precise point following the punch line. Jokes are told as "understanding tests," since not everyone necessarily gets every joke, and getting the joke involves certain items of background knowledge and rational processing. Thus the absence of laughter immediately upon the completion of a joke becomes significant either as a sign of disapproval or as a failure to understand. Recipients may thus produce mirthless laughter at the proper juncture with the dual aim of demonstrating understanding *and* a lack of appreciation, which consequently constitutes an attack on the teller.

Sherzer, though not a practitioner of Conversation Analysis as such, elaborates on work by Sacks in ways which make him most logically fit at this point in our review. He analyzes both unconscious, unnoticed puns and conscious, purposeful puns (1978). He shows how the unconscious puns, like *Baloney, you don't eat meat!,* contribute to cohesion in discourse, while the conscious ones disrupt the cohesion of the discourse and break the current frame or change the topic. Thus speech play is centrifugal with relation to the discourse. At the same time, from an interactional perspective, puns can serve a number of functions such as changing the topic, getting the floor, and relieving tension, though they may cause problems which require special comment, correction, or apology. These interrelated tendencies appear in many examples analyzed in the body of this book. Sherzer (1985) builds on Sacks's analysis of jokes as understanding tests, and consequently as forms of aggression directed at the audience, as well as some third party, namely the *butt* of the joke. The recipient of a joke typically laughs at the crucial point, while the recipient of a pun often groans as a sign of understanding. Finally, Sherzer points out that jokes contain a third sort of interactional aggression as well, since we use them to gain and hold the floor.

Schegloff (1987) notes that utterances may be ambiguous as to whether they were produced seriously or nonseriously. On the one hand, we may claim to have produced as nonserious even serious utterances, for instance by saying *I was just kidding;* and on the other hand, a listener may insist on hearing the serious import of a joking utterance. Sometimes speakers use what Schegloff calls a joke-first practice in response to the first part of an adjacency pair, a story, an experience, or any utterance which ordinarily requires a direct reply. The practice involves doing a joke first, that is before producing the sequentially relevant turn. These joke-firsts usually take the form of intentional misunderstandings in which the second speaker reanalyzes the foregoing utterance in a manner at odds with the current context. They often play on an ambiguity or vagueness in a particular word or phrase, and hence depend not only on a particular semantic content but also on a particular lexical form, as in the traditional punning reply in the pair below, which involves a pretended misunderstanding of *say* 'indicate' as opposed to *say* 'utter'. This example illustrates punning based on the discrepancy between compositional and idiomatic interpretations for a single turn.

A: What does your watch say?
B: Ticktock, ticktock.

The associated sort of role-play, in which a conversationalist pretends to have misunderstood an utterance in order to produce a skewed response to a reanalyzed version of it, provides the basis for spontaneous punning. Once the pretended misunderstanding is recognized as a joke and prompts a small laugh, its speaker usually returns to the serious mode and gives an appropriate response. We may reverse the strategy and pretend to misunderstand an attempted joke, treating it as a legitimate misinterpretation and thus refusing to accept it as a joke at all. As Schegloff, Jefferson, and Sacks (1977) also note, conversationalists may exploit the normal format for other-correction to make a joke such as, "Not fondly, fond*ling*." And this means another standard reflex within the turn-taking mechanism is available for joking. Examples treated in the preceding chapters show various other ways we commandeer regular conversational devices for joking purposes.

In a recent publication in the Conversation Analysis vein,

Wilson (1989) places jokes and banter among the "out-modes" or types of talk separate from conversation proper. For Wilson, jokes are either narratives or riddles built around ethnic stereotypes; he says of both that they are sets of turns intended to amuse listeners, though this characterization would include all types of stories and other performances as well. Further, Wilson defines banter quite narrowly to apply only to apparent verbal attacks on other participants. This leaves most of the joking described in the present book still within conversation proper, since it ranges from personal anecdotes to irony, self-effacing jibes, verbal attacks on nonparticipants, puns, and so on, which means Wilson's remarks provide no help for a general approach to humor in everyday talk. Moreover, treating canned jokes and banter as events separate from conversation per se suggests a discontinuity where none is registered by conversationalists themselves, since narrative jokes routinely fade into the allusion on one side and into the personal anecdote on the other.

By way of summarizing this section, we have seen that laughter has multiple functions in conversation. It may signal nervousness, resistance to troubles, and nonserious intent as well as genuine hilarity. Moreover, laughter serves to mark topic boundaries and to transition into new topics. Sacks and Sherzer provide useful analyses of puns and jokes, focusing on their internal organization and integration into the conversational context, while stressing their test function in the interpersonal domain. Finally, Schegloff has identified a joke-first practice constructed around the adjacency pair itself, the very basis of conversational organization. Perhaps more important than any specific conclusion, however, is the methodological significance of work in Conversation Analysis with its detailed analyses at the micro-level of conversational organization.

Conclusions

To summarize this review as a whole, multiple perspectives on humor over the centuries result in an interesting but incomplete picture of joking in everyday talk, particularly because so little work on humor has considered genuine conversation, and work on conversation has rarely treated joking as such. Too often the term *humor* covers narrative jokes, funny stories, punning, irony, teasing, and flippant utterances generally; this renders statements about the relation of humor to social control, aggression, rapport, and similar matters difficult to assess. Poking fun at errors has a clearer social control function than has wordplay; sarcasm apparently conveys more aggression than does telling narrative jokes; participation in a round of relating funny personal anecdotes enhances rapport far more than do ironic comments, and so on. We need to look more closely at individual joking sequences in particular contexts to determine degrees of aggression and testing, their relation to positive and negative politeness, the play frame and customary joking relationships. The investigation of real joking contexts in the preceding chapters revealed types of joking not mentioned in the literature on humor, as well as mixed forms and interrelations between the genres usually recognized. Its focus on the concrete contexts of humor helps answer questions about the role of the listener, the extent and kinds of audience participation; it shows how we lead into narrative jokes and wordplay, how they turn into rounds of joke telling or banter, and how they segue back into serious talk. And this, in turn, sheds new light on the organization of conversation itself, the development and maintenance of topical cohesion, rapport, and interaction generally. The variety and popularity of canned humor along with the frequency and persistence of spontaneous joking in everyday talk suggest that conversation often aims less at the expeditious exchange of information than at pleasant interaction, especially between friends in social settings, and particularly for those who enjoy a customary joking relationship.

References

Akmajian, Adrian; Richard A. Demers; and Robert M. Harnish. 1984. *Linguistics: An introduction to language and communication,* 2nd ed. Cambridge, MA: MIT Press.

Apte, Mahadev L. 1983. Humor research, methodology and theory in anthropology. In *Handbook of humor research,* vol. 1, ed. by P. E. McGhee and J. H. Goldstein, 183–212. New York: Springer.

———. 1985. *Humor and laughter.* Ithaca: Cornell University Press.

———. 1987. Ethnic humor versus 'sense of humor'. *American Behavioral Scientist* 30. 27–41.

Bateson, Gregory. 1953. The position of humor in human communication. In *Cybernetics, ninth conference,* ed. by H. von Foerster, 1–47. New York: Josiah Macy, Jr. Foundation.

———. 1954 (1972). A theory of play and fantasy. In *Steps to an ecology of mind,* ed. by G. Bateson, 177–93. San Francisco: Chandler.

———. 1956 (1972). Toward a theory of schizophrenia. In *Steps to an ecology of mind,* ed. by G. Bateson, 201–27. San Francisco: Chandler.

———. 1969 (1972). Metalogue: What is an instinct? In *Steps to an ecology of mind,* ed. by G. Bateson, 38–58. San Francisco: Chandler.

Bauman, Richard. 1986. *Story, performance, and event.* Cambridge: Cambridge University Press.

Bergson, Henri. 1899 (1911). *Laughter: An essay on the meaning of the comic.* New York: Macmillan.

Brown, James. 1956. Eight types of pun. *P.M.L.A.* 71. 14–26.

Brown, Penelope, and Stephen Levinson. 1978. Universals in language usage: Politeness phenomena. In *Questions and politeness,* ed. by E. N. Goody, 56–310. Cambridge: Cambridge University Press. [Reissued as: *Politeness: Some universals in language usage.* Cambridge: Cambridge University Press, 1987.]

Chapman, Anton J. 1983. Humor and laughter in social interaction and some implications. In *Handbook of humor research,* vol. 1, ed. by P. E. McGhee and J. H. Goldstein, 135–57. New York: Springer.

Chapman, Anton J., and Hugh C. Foot (eds.). 1976. *Humor and laughter: Theory, research and applications.* London: Wiley.

———. 1977. *It's a funny thing, humor.* Oxford: Pergamon.

Clark, Herbert H., and Richard J. Gerrig. 1984. On the pretense theory of irony. *Journal of Experimental Psychology: General* 113. 121–26.

Coser, Rose L. 1960. Laughter among colleagues. *Psychiatry* 23. 81–95.

Culler, Jonathan. 1988. The call of the phoneme: Introduction. In *On puns,* ed. by J. Culler, 1–16. Oxford: Blackwell.

Cutler, Anne. 1974. On saying what you mean without meaning what you say. Papers from the tenth regional meeting of the Chicago Linguistic Society, 117–27.

Derrida, Jacques. 1974. *Glas.* Paris: Editions Galilee.

Douglas, Mary. 1968. The social control of cognition. *Man* 3. 361–76.

Duranti, Alessandro. 1986. The audience as co-author: An introduction. *Text* 6, 3. 239–47.

Eastman, Max. 1936. *Enjoyment of laughter.* New York: Simon and Schuster.

Farb, Peter. 1973. *Word play.* New York: Knopf.

Fine, Gary Alan. 1983. Sociological approaches to the study of humor. In *Handbook of humor research,* vol. 1, ed. by P. E. McGhee and J. H. Goldstein, 159–81. New York: Springer.

Freud, Sigmund. 1905 (1960). *Jokes and their relation to the unconscious.* New York: Norton.

Fry, William F., Jr. 1963. *Sweet madness: A study of humor.* Palo Alto: Pacific Books.

Goffman, Erving. 1955. On face-work. *Psychiatry* 18, 3. 213–31. [Reprinted in: E. Goffman. 1967. *Interaction ritual.* Chicago: Aldine, 5–45.]

———. 1959. *The presentation of self in everyday life.* Garden City: Anchor Books.

———. 1961. *Encounters.* Indianapolis: Bobbs-Merrill.

———. 1967. *Interaction ritual.* Chicago: Aldine.

———. 1974. *Frame analysis.* Cambridge, MA: Harvard University Press.

Goldstein, Jeffrey H., and Paul E. McGhee (eds.). 1972. *The psychology of humor.* New York: Academic Press.

Goodchilds, Jacqueline D. 1972. On being witty: Causes, correlates and consequences. In *The psychology of humor,* ed. by J. H. Goldstein and P. E. McGhee, 173–93. New York: Academic Press.

Goodwin, Charles. 1986. Audience diversity, participation and interpretation. *Text* 6, 3. 283–316.

Goody, Esther N. 1978. Introduction. In *Questions and politeness,* ed. by E. N. Goody, 1–16. Cambridge: Cambridge University Press.

Grice, H. P. 1967 (1975). Logic and conversation. In *Syntax and semantics,* vol. 3: *Speech acts,* ed. by P. Cole and J. L. Morgan, 41–58. New York: Academic Press.

———. 1978. Further notes on logic and conversation. In *Syntax and semantics,* vol. 9: *Pragmatics,* ed. by P. Cole, 113–27. New York: Academic.

Gumperz, John J. 1982a. *Discourse strategies.* Cambridge: Cambridge University Press.

———. 1982b. The linguistic bases of communicative competence. In *Analyzing discourse: Text and talk* (Georgetown University

Roundtable on Languages and Linguistics 1981), ed. by D. Tannen, 323–34. Washington, DC: Georgetown University Press.

Halliday, M. A. K. 1976. *System and function in language.* London: Oxford University Press.

———. 1978. *Language as social semiotic.* London: Edward Arnold.

Hobbes, Thomas. 1650 (1840). *Human nature (The English works of Thomas Hobbes,* vol. 4). London: John Bohn.

———. 1651 (1909). *Leviathan.* London: Oxford University Press.

Hockett, Charles F. 1960 (1977). Jokes. In *The view from language,* ed. by C. F. Hockett, 257–89. Athens, GA: University of Georgia Press.

Hopper, Paul. 1988. Emergent grammar and the a priori grammar postulate. In *Linguistics in context,* ed. by D. Tannen, 117–34. Norwood, NJ: Ablex.

Hutcheson, Francis. 1750 (1971). *Reflections on laughter.* New York: Garland.

Hymes, Dell. 1962. The ethnography of speaking. In *Anthropology and human behavior,* ed. by T. Gladwin and W. C. Sturtevant, 13–53. Washington, DC: The Anthropology Society of Washington.

———. 1972. Models of the interaction of language and social life. In *Directions in sociolinguistics,* ed. by J. J. Gumperz and D. Hymes, 35–71. New York: Holt, Rinehart and Winston.

———. 1974. *Foundations of sociolinguistics.* Philadelphia: University of Pennsylvania Press.

Jakobson, Roman. 1960. Closing statement: Linguistics and poetics. In *Style in language,* ed. by T. Sebeok, 350–77. Cambridge, MA: MIT Press.

Jefferson, Gail. 1972. Side sequences. In *Studies in social interaction,* ed. by D. Sudnow, 294–338. New York: Free Press.

———. 1978. Sequential aspects of storytelling in conversation. In *Studies in the organization of conversational interaction,* ed. by J. Schenkein, 219–48. New York: Academic Press.

———. 1979. A technique for inviting laughter and its subsequent acceptance/declination. In *Everyday language: Studies in ethnomethodology,* ed. by G. Psathas, 79–96. New York: Irvington.

———. 1984a. On the organization of laughter in talk about troubles. In *Structures of social action,* ed. by J. M. Atkinson and J. Heritage, 346–69. Cambridge: Cambridge University Press.

———. 1984b. On stepwise transition from talk about a trouble to inappropriately next-positioned matters. In *Structures of social action,* ed. by J. M. Atkinson and J. Heritage, 191–222. Cambridge: Cambridge University Press.

———. 1985. An exercise in the transcription and analysis of laughter. In *Handbook of discourse analysis,* vol. 3: *Discourse and dialogue,* ed. by T. A. van Dijk, 25–34. London: Academic Press.

Jefferson, Gail; Harvey Sacks; and Emanuel A. Schegloff. 1976. Some notes on laughing together. Pragmatics Microfiche 1.8: A2. Cambridge: Cambridge University Department of Linguistics.

Kane, Thomas R.; Jerry Suls; and James Tedeschi. 1977. Humor as a tool of social interaction. In *It's a funny thing, humor,* ed. by A. J. Chapman and H. C. Foot, 13–16. Oxford: Pergamon.

Kant, Immanuel. 1790 (1951). *Critique of judgment.* New York: Hafner.

Kaufer, David S. 1981. Understanding ironic communication. *Journal of Pragmatics* 5. 495–510.

Kirshenblatt-Gimblett, Barbara (ed.). 1976. *Speech play.* Philadelphia: University of Pennsylvania Press.

Koestler, Arthur. 1964. *The act of creation.* New York: Macmillan.

Kolek, Leszek S. 1985. Toward a poetics of comic narratives: Notes on the semiotic structure of jokes. *Semiotica* 53. 145–63.

Labov, William, and Joshua Waletzky. 1967. Narrative analysis: Oral versions of personal experience. In *Essays on the verbal and visual arts,* ed. by June Helm, 12–44. Seattle: University of Washington Press.

La Fave, Lawrence. 1977. Ethnic humor: From paradoxes toward principles. In *It's a funny thing, humor,* ed. by A. J. Chapman and H. C. Foot, 273–60. Oxford: Pergamon.

La Fave, Lawrence; Jay Haddad; and William A. Maesen. 1976. Superiority, enhanced self-esteem and perceived incongruity humor theory. In *Humor and laughter: Theory, research and applications,* ed. by A. J. Chapman and H. C. Foot, 63–91. London: Wiley.

La France, Marianne. 1983. Felt versus feigned funniness: Issues in coding smiling and laughter. In *Handbook of humor research,* vol. 1, ed. by P. E. McGhee and J. H. Goldstein, 1–12. New York: Springer.

Lakoff, Robin. 1973. The logic of politeness; or, minding your p's and q's. *Papers from the ninth regional meeting of the Chicago Linguistic Society,* 292–305.

———. 1977. What you can do with words: Politeness, pragmatics, and performatives. In *Proceedings of the Texas conference on performatives, presuppositions and implicatures,* ed. by A. Rogers, B. Wall, and J. P. Murphy, 79–105. Washington, DC: Center for Applied Linguistics.

———. 1982. Persuasive discourse and ordinary conversation, with examples from advertising. In *Analyzing discourse: Text and talk* (Georgetown University Roundtable on Languages and Linguistics 1981), ed. by D. Tannen, 25–42. Washington, DC: Georgetown University Press.

———. 1990. *Talking power: The politics of language in our lives.* New York: Basic Books.

Legman, G. 1968 (1982). *No laughing matter.* Bloomington: Indiana University Press.

Lehrer, Adrienne. 1983. *Wine and conversation.* Bloomington: Indiana University Press.

Linstead, Steve. 1988. 'Jokers wild': Humor in organizational culture. In

Humor in society, ed. by C. Powell and G. E. C. Paton, 123–48. New York: St. Martin's Press.

Lorenz, Konrad. 1963 (1966). *On aggression.* New York: Harcourt, Brace & World.

Malkiel, Yakov. 1959. Studies in irreversible binomials. *Lingua* 8. 113–60.

Martineau, William H. 1972. A model of the social functions of humor. In *The psychology of humor,* ed. by J. H. Goldstein and P. E. McGhee, 101–25. New York: Academic Press.

McGhee, Paul E. 1979. *Humor: Its origin and development.* San Francisco: Freeman.

McGhee, Paul E., and Antony J. Chapman (eds.) 1980. *Children's humor.* Chichester: Wiley.

McGhee, Paul E., and Jeffrey H. Goldstein (eds.). 1983. *Handbook of humor research,* 2 vols. New York: Springer.

Milner, George B. 1972. Homo ridens: Toward a semiotic theory of humor and laughter. *Semiotica* 5. 1–30.

Mindess, Harvey. 1971. *Laughter and liberation.* Los Angeles: Nash.

Morreall, John. 1983. *Taking laughter seriously.* Albany: State University of New York Press.

———. (ed.) 1987. *The philosophy of laughter and humor.* Albany: State Univesity of New York Press.

———. 1990. Prepared versus spontaneous humor. unpublished manuscript.

Nash, Walter. 1985. *The language of humor: Style and technique in comic discourse.* London: Longman.

Norrick, Neal R. 1984. Stock conversational witticisms. *Journal of Pragmatics* 8. 195–209.

———. 1986. A frame-theoretical analysis of verbal humor: Bisociation as schema conflict. *Semiotica* 60. 225–45.

———. 1987. From wit to comedy: Bisociation and intertextuality. *Semiotica* 61. 113–25.

———. 1988. Binomial meaning in texts. *Journal of English Linguistics* 21, 1. 72–87.

———. 1989. Intertextuality in humor. *Humor* 2. 117–39.

———. 1993a. Repetition in canned jokes and spontaneous conversational joking. *Humor* 5. to appear.

———. 1993b. Repetition as a conversational joking strategy. In *Repetition in discourse,* ed. by B. Johnstone. Norwood: Ablex, to appear.

Philips, Susan U. 1975. Teasing, punning, and putting people on. Working Papers in Sociolinguistics 28, December 1975.

Pilcher, William W. 1972. *The Portland longshoremen.* New York: Holt, Rinehart and Winston.

Polanyi, Livia. 1979. So what's the point? *Semiotica* 25. 207–41.

Pollio, Howard R. 1983. Notes toward a field theory of humor. In *Hand-*

book of humor research, vol. 1, ed. by P. E. McGhee and J. H. Goldstein, 213–30. New York: Springer.

Radcliff-Brown, Alfred R. 1940. On joking relationships. *Africa* 13. 195–210.

Raskin, Victor. 1985. *Semantic mechanisms of humor.* Dordrecht: Reidel.

Redfern, Walter. 1984. *Puns.* London: Blackwell.

Richter, Jean Paul. 1804. *Vorschule der Ästhetik* (Werke, Band 5). Munich: Carl Hanser.

Ryave, Alan L. 1978. On the achievement of a series of stories. In *Studies in the organization of conversational interaction,* ed. by J. Schenkein, 113–32. New York: Academic Press.

Sacks, Harvey. 1972. On the analyzability of stories by children. In *Directions in sociolinguistics,* ed. by J. J. Gumperz and D. Hymes, 325–45. New York: Holt, Rinehart and Winston.

———. 1973. On some puns with some intimations. In *Report of the twenty-third annual roundtable meeting in linguistics and language studies,* ed. by R. W. Shuy, 135–44. Washington, DC: Georgetown University Press.

———. 1974. An analysis of the course of a joke's telling. In *Explorations in the ethnography of speaking,* ed. by R. Bauman and J. Sherzer, 337–53. Cambridge: Cambridge University Press.

Saussure, Ferdinand de. 1916 (1966). *Course in general linguistics.* New York: McGraw-Hill.

Schegloff, Emanuel A. 1968. Sequencing in conversational openings. *American Anthropologist* 70. 1075–95.

———. 1982. Discourse as an interactional achievement: Some uses of 'uh huh' and other things that come between sentences. In *Analyzing discourse: Text and talk* (Georgetown University Roundtable on Languages and Linguistics 1981), ed. by D. Tannen, 71–93. Washington, DC: Georgetown University Press.

———. 1987. Some sources of misunderstanding in talk-in-interaction. *Linguistics* 25. 201–18.

———. 1988. Discourse as an interactional achievement II: An exercise in conversational analysis. In *Linguistics in context,* ed. by D. Tannen, 135–58. Norwood: Ablex.

Schegloff, Emanuel A., and Harvey Sacks. 1973. Opening up closings. *Semiotica* 7,4. 289–327.

Schegloff, Emanuel A.; Gail Jefferson; and Harvey Sacks. 1977. The preference for self-correction in the organization of repair in conversation. *Language* 53. 361–82.

Schenkein, James N. 1972. Towards an analysis of natural conversation and the sense of *heheh. Semiotica* 6. 344–77.

Schiffrin, Deborah. 1984. Jewish argument as sociability. *Language in Society* 13. 311–35.

———. 1987. *Discourse markers.* Cambridge: Cambridge University Press.

Schutz, Charles E. 1989. The sociability of ethnic jokes. *Humor* 2, 2. 165–77.

Sharrock, W. W., and Roy Turner. 1978. On a conversational environment for equivocality. In *Studies in the organization of conversational interaction,* ed. by J. Schenkein, 173–97. New York: Academic Press.

Sherzer, Joel. 1978. Oh! That's a pun and I didn't mean it. *Semiotica* 22. 335–50.

———. 1985. Puns and jokes. In *Handbook of discourse analysis,* vol. 3: *Discourse and dialogue,* ed. by T. A. van Dijk, 213–21. London: Academic Press.

Sperber, Dan. 1984. Verbal irony: pretense or echoic mention? *Journal of Experimental Psychology: General* 113. 130–36.

Sperber, Dan, and Deirdre Wilson. 1981. Irony and the use/mention distinction. In *Radical pragmatics,* ed. by P. Cole. New York: Academic Press.

Spielman, Roger W. 1987. Collateral information in narrative discourse. *Journal of Literary Semantics* 16, 3. 200–26.

Sully, James. 1902. *An essay on laughter.* New York: Longmans, Green.

Suls, Jerry. 1983. Cognitive processes in humor appreciation. In *Handbook of humor research,* vol. 1, ed. by P. E. McGhee and J. H. Goldstein, 39–57. New York: Springer.

Swift, Jonathan. 1719 (1801). *The art of punning* (*Works,* vol. 8). London: Nichols.

Sykes, A. J. M. 1966. Joking relationships in an industrial setting. *American Anthropologist* 68. 188–93.

Tannen, Deborah. 1984. *Conversational style.* Norwood, NJ: Ablex.

———. 1986. *That's not what I meant!* New York: Morrow.

———. 1987. Repetition in conversation: Toward a poetics of talk. *Language* 63. 574–605.

———. 1989. *Talking voices: Repetition, dialogue, and imagery in conversational discourse.* Cambridge: Cambridge University Press.

———. 1990. *You just don't understand.* New York: Morrow.

Whitehead, Alfred N., and Bertrand Russell. 1910–13 (1960). *Principia mathematica.* Cambridge: Cambridge University Press.

Wilson, Christopher P. 1979. *Jokes: Form, content, use, and function.* London: Academic Press.

Wilson, John. 1989. *On the boundaries of conversation.* Oxford: Pergamon.

Yamaguchi, Haruhiko. 1988. How to pull strings with words: Deceptive violations in the garden-path joke. *Journal of Pragmatics* 12. 323–37.

Ziv, Abner. 1984. *Personality and sense of humor.* New York: Springer.

Index

Author

NEAL R. NORRICK is Professor of English Linguistics at Northern Illinois University and author of *How Proverbs Mean* and *Semiotic Principles in Semantic Theory.* His research interests include conversation, verbal humor, pragmatics, semantics, and poetics.